S0-BLS-948

*An Inspirational Journey into
the Life, Legacy, and Influence of
Billy Barty*

*Within
Reach*

Michael and Debra Copeland

PRESS

Copyright © 2002 by Michael and Debra Copeland

Within Reach
by Michael and Debra Copeland

Printed in the United States of America

Library of Congress Control Number: 2002114808
ISBN 1-591603-91-9

All rights reserved. No part of this publication may be reproduced or transmitted in any form or by any means without written permission of the publisher.

Unless otherwise indicated, Bible quotations are taken from the King James Version.

Xulon Press
11350 Random Hills Road
Suite 800
Fairfax, VA 22030
(703) 279-6511
XulonPress.com

To order additional copies, call 1-866-909-BOOK (2665).

CELEBRITY QUOTES

George Lucas: "Billy Barty is a man who has touched so many lives with entertainment and joy. His achievements have certainly inspired all of us."

Mickey Rooney: "I'm proud to have known Billy. I am proud to know that 'God' has let Billy entertain and gave him the talent that he alone possessed. For it is not how 'Big' you are; it's what you do with it. Billy has done more than you could ever see."

Tommy Lasorda: "Although he was small in stature, he was big in character."

Pat Boone: "It was so typical of Billy, anything to help out a friend."

Peter Marshall: "I loved Billy very much and think of him often, which always brings a smile to my face."

Ed Asner: "I've always loved Billy Barty with his warmth and his giving."

Bob Barker: "The loss of this little man leaves a big void in our lives."

Betty White: "Billy was a good friend for more years than I can count."

Willie Aames: "It is hard NOT to have been touched by Billy in some way."

Fred Travalena: "Billy was a gift to all who knew him."

Dick Clark: "Words cannot describe my total admiration for Billy Barty."

Dick Van Patten: "I miss him very much, and aside from his talent, he was also a very wonderful man."

Peter Falk: "There are some terrific people in the world, and Billy was one of them."

Kent McCray: "When he came to work, he came prepared. He was always there and you never had to find him. He was a professional from the word go."

Johnny Whitaker: "Billy taught me the greatest things about comedy and timing and the importance of being a true entertainer."

WE HONOR

Dr. C. Wesley Morse and Dede Barty Morse

*We would like to give special honor to Dede Barty Morse
and to Dr. C. Wesley Morse whose kindness and generosity
cannot be measured. For without their love and support,
this book would have never materialized.*

DEDICATION

We give our thanks and appreciation to all those who have participated in sending us their thoughts, sentiments, and stories to make this book an everlasting tribute to Billy Barty.

Even though the producers of this book are of a Christian belief, the people who contributed their expressions for the formation of this book may represent many religious faiths. One thing remains consistent, however, and that is the fact that Billy Barty left behind inspiration, hope, endurance, and love.

We would like to give recognition to the Barty, Morse, Neilson, Copeland, Timpany, Ungaro, Piper, and Maglione families.

The Billy Barty Foundation; the Little People of America; Debra's mother Nancy Ungaro; our children Jennifer, Stasia, and Joe; and the celebrities, fans, and friends listed in the contents of this book. We send a special thank you to our granddaughter Tiffany, who has kept us going with her unconditional love.

Note: The order of sequence in the table of contents does not imply one person's importance more than the other, and therefore we hold all who have taken the time to selflessly participate in this book in high esteem.

GREATER LOVE

He stood for others like he was ten feet tall.
Though his body had pain, and in height he was small.
His spirit was strong as the obstacles came.
He fought in the battle to give others a name.
It's not the height of a person that makes one great.
But rather the heart if it loves or it hates.
Seeing the virtue that came from his life,
Should encourage us all to endure what is right.
And when we're discouraged there were shoes left behind.
From a big hearted giant who made a better mankind.
Though our sizes are different his shoes we can wear.
And walk in the footsteps that God has held dear.
Debra Copeland ©2002

Greater love hath no man than this, that a man lay down his life for his friends. (John 15:13)

This book is not a biography. You can look for Billy's autobiography written by Linda Jones (Spike Jones' daughter) in the future.

A portion of the royalties from this book will be donated to the south Florida chapter of the organization, Little People of America.

"A LESSON IN COMPASSION"

By Debra Copeland

During the Christmas holiday season in 2001, Michael and I were taking our granddaughter Tiffany to a theme park out in Orlando, Florida. A spectacular event was scheduled, and we were all looking forward to a particular concert with singing, drama, and fireworks. But we had a problem. I became physically afflicted and was unable to stand in the park.

As the announcer stated over the loudspeaker that the festivities would begin in ten minutes, masses of people gathered around us. We were blessed to have found a bench to sit on earlier, but it was hard to see what was going on as everyone else was standing up.

So, trying to not disappoint our granddaughter, I encouraged my husband to do whatever he could so that Tiffany would have a memorable time and enjoy the atmosphere.

While everyone was waiting in suspense for the excitement to begin, all of a sudden I felt as if I was in the movie *Scrooge*. Most of us have seen the part where the angel took Scrooge to look over his past. Even though my story is basically different, I began feeling sorry for myself. I wanted to be part of the celebration, and now I was surrounded by what appeared to me to be some very pushy people who were overly caught up in the moment.

But even in my grinch-like state, it was as though an invisible angel was about to open my eyes and let me see what was truly set before me. I glanced up and saw someone across the way from where I was sitting. There was a young woman (I would say in her twenties) in a wheelchair, shoved in the corner and out of the shadow of the crowd.

Her loved one was gently laying his hands on her leg, and it appeared to me as if he was praying for her. He didn't seem to be very interested in the performance that was about to take place, but rather concerned that the woman he was with was made more comfortable.

Since I wasn't able to stand, it was a wonder I could see anything through the billowing mounds of tall people.

Then I thought about Billy and all the people who were of short stature. So this is a sample of what it feels like to be small? I learned you can see a lot of things when you are small, things that others miss by being insensitive.

Beginning to understand a little bit of what God must observe through this situation, I came away with much more than a few moments of entertainment. Not being able to do what others were doing gave me a new level of *compassion*.

As we were approaching the end of the performance, the thundering footsteps of a multitude of people running and shoving each other trying to see the last act of the musical were rather amusing to me. You see, the musical was centered on Jesus being born to save mankind from their sins.

Live camels proceeded down an entryway, with Mary, Joseph, and the wise men bringing gifts to the baby Jesus.

When others saw the procession, I honestly thought I was going to be trampled underfoot. There was a lot of confusion about what road the performers were to travel down, and I literally held on to the bench hoping I would come out alive after everything was over.

While this is not a blot at all against the theme park, it does show the nature of man. Then it really hit me.

What if I had been born with a handicap?

This discrimination is what Billy fought so hard against. He wanted to show the world that the disabled and little folks have much to offer us. They have a deepness and sensitivity that many people of average height lack. They feel with their hearts, and it is unfortunate today that many people have let their hearts grow cold.

While working on this book, we were told that a few people were upset with the way Billy handled his influence. They had felt that he could have done more for them, but they never realized how much this kind man was doing behind the scenes.

There will always be critics, and Billy learned early on that you have to continue with what you know to be right, even in the midst of opposition. Mistakes will be made, but there is not one person on this earth who hasn't made any. We all fall *short,* so to speak.

To Billy, everyone mattered, known or unknown. That is what made him such a "Big Man" in many eyes, even though at the time of his death he was only 3'9".

INTRODUCTION

When my wife Debra and I started to put together my Uncle Billy's website in 1997, we also started to help him with his fan mail correspondence.

Along with the standard requests for autographed pictures from Billy, there were some very touching personal stories from fans. Many had commented on how much of an impact Billy had made on their lives. The outpouring of love inspired us to test the waters, so to speak, and to see if there were others who had stories, recollections, and sentiments regarding Billy that they also would like to share. We felt the need to show how Billy used his success in entertainment to positively influence other important areas of life, for instance, in being an advocate for the disabled.

Hence, after a lengthy battle to answer the question "What's the title of the book going to be?" the answer came to me while recalling one of life's main goals for my 3'9" uncle. That goal was to bring this world within reach to those of short stature. The more I thought about the title *Within Reach,* the more aspects of his life I could relate it to. Of course, his philosophy "You've Got to Think Big," and the song by the same name, inspired many to reach for a better self image. We hope this book reflects my uncle's overcoming spirit and encourages all who read it to see that our goals in life are always within reach.

Michael Copeland

CONTENTS

Contents

Chapter One

DEDE BARTY MORSE

Albert, Ellen, Evelyn, Dede, and Billy Barty.
Photo courtesy of Dede Barty Morse

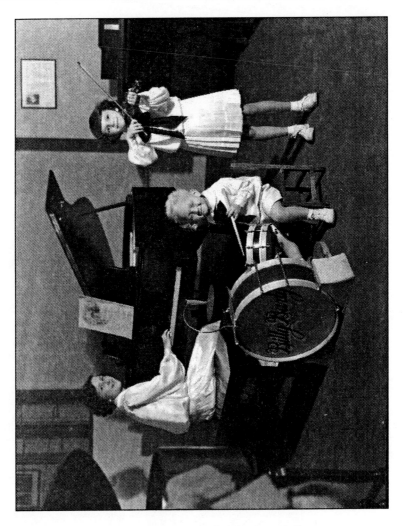

*Evelyn on piano, Dede playing violin,
and Billy playing drums.
Photo courtesy of Dede Barty Morse*

MEMORIES FROM DEDE
Dede Barty Morse

After leaving Pennsylvania, our mother and father moved to Los Angeles, California, where they resided in the same house for over forty-five years. In our house we had a living and dining room, hall, kitchen, breakfast room, three bedrooms, and one bathroom.

The latter (the bathroom) always caused much confusion and yelling with my brother Billy, my sister Evelyn, and me.

Oriental carpets covered the polished hardwood floors in the living room and adjoining dining room. Over the never-used fireplace in the living room were family pictures of various shapes and sizes, making a decorative display from one end of the mantel to the other, each telling a story.

The upright piano on the opposite wall had been the gathering place for many sing-alongs. Background music played by my sister Evelyn or our friends always set the tempo of the favorite dance steps of that era.

I still remember my four-month-old granddaughter Jessica entertaining her great-grandparents twenty-four years ago as she was sitting in her Jolly Jumping swing. Her little feet were creating their own original dance steps, while her great-aunt played some of that background music again in the same room.

The kitchen was our mother's favorite room. She loved to cook and the words "Are you hungry?" and "Let me fix you something" had been her way of giving to others all her life. I recall our father spending time at his little desk in his bedroom, reading the *Wall Street Journal* and other publications, trying to keep the rust out of his eighty-six-year-old mind.

Our parents had been married over sixty-one years and courted (as they called it) for five years before that. It was comforting to know that in their twilight years they could call on a memory from any direction in their cherished home.

There were times when traveling on the road that we stayed in large homes on a lot of acreage. They would call them Bed and Breakfasts now. In the dining room of these homes you would sit and eat with other people. This had to be done so that they could survive and keep their houses up because the taxes were so high.

Learning about Prejudice

Because we were raised as Catholics, we would find ourselves going to confession in one town and going to Mass in another. One Sunday we went to Mass in the deep south and some African Americans were standing outside of the church. I thought to myself at a very young age, "Is God black or white?" and "Why are these people standing outside of the church?"

That was the first time I learned about prejudice and segregation, and I felt really saddened by it.

Billy as a Humanitarian

It was in Kentucky when we were touring as our vaudeville act "Billy Barty and Sisters" that Billy began to have a humanitarian instinct as well as a deep interest in sports, which stayed with him all through his life.

Christmas morning in 1935 in Louisville, the family started out to do a benefit at the local orphanage. When we were a few blocks from our hotel, Billy shouted that he had left something behind and needed it badly.

So the car went back to the hotel, and in went Billy. Minutes later he emerged with a football, saying, "Some kid might like to play a little football with me."

Ellen, Evelyn, Dede, and Billy.
Photo courtesy of Dede Barty Morse

Albert Barty and young Billy

Photo courtesy of Dede Barty Morse

*Photo collage of Billy, Dede, and Evelyn with
their act "Billy Barty and Sisters"
Photo courtesy of Dede Barty Morse*

Photo collage of Karl Moldrum's Baby Orchestra.
Photo courtesy of Dede Barty Morse

LOS ANGELES CITY COLLEGE
Dede Barty Morse and Dr. C. Wesley Morse

When the family returned to Los Angeles in late 1941, it became apparent that World War II would end Vaudeville. It was time for Billy to finish high school and go to college.

In high school, he played all the sports he could. Later, he and Max Fine and Jerry Brown founded a magazine called *High School on Parade* for which Billy was the sports editor. It gave him a taste of writing, which he enjoyed, coupled with his great love: sports.

In college at LACC, he majored in journalism, thinking he would perhaps find a niche as a sports announcer or writer. He finished his formal education at LA State College, the successor to LACC, and there he lettered in basketball and football. In November of 1945, he played in an exhibition football game between LACC and UCLA's freshman squad at the Los Angeles Coliseum. He received a standing ovation from the crowd when he caught a seventeen-yard pass in a play especially designed for him. He was awarded an honorary doctorate in letters in 1996 by this same alma mater, now Los Angeles State University.

Paisano Newsletter

Herb Berkus

In June of 1943, I graduated from high school and immediately joined the Navy. There was a waiting period of about five months before I was to report to boot camp. I enrolled at LA City College to take a few courses. It was there that I met Billy.

There wasn't any organized football because of wartime restrictions, so a group of us formed our own teams and Billy was on mine. During one of our games, I sustained a knee injury and Billy carried me off the field unassisted.

A few years ago, I met him at a performance of the LA Junior Philharmonic Orchestra, where he was a guest, and I reminded him of the incident. He was ecstatic, proclaiming that all of his life he had been telling people that he played college football and no one believed him. Now here I was, living proof that he did play college football. He was a wonderful athlete and a wonderful person.

Morris Schulatsky

At 3'9" tall, he was the smallest man ever to win letters in football and basketball. He could run the 100–yard dash in 14.6. He could long jump 13 feet. He played golf and could lift his weight with barbells, but for his acting roles afterward and for his philanthropies for "little people," Billy Barty was big.

Arnie Gordon

I attended Los Angeles City College after World War II, from 1947–1950. I was features editor of the college newspaper, the *Collegian*, right after Billy had been advertising manager. I eventually became Associated Students Vice-President.

I would like to add my testimonial to the fact that Billy Barty did indeed play college football on the college's regular varsity team.

They would give him the football and then pick him up and throw him over the line of the scrimmage to the stunned amazement of the other team.

We all miss him very much.

*Billy in cap and gown, graduating from Los Angeles City College.
Photo courtesy of Dede Barty Morse*

AMERICA

Billy was very active in the Republican Party, but as a humanitarian he never asked people whether they were Democrat, Republican, or Independent because he really loved America and wanted to keep peace. I am glad he was spared the 9–11 tragedy as it would have devastated him.

When my granddaughter Jessica was about nine or ten, we were visiting Washington, D.C., and I asked her what she would like to see while we were in town. She said, "The White House!" So I called my brother Billy to see if he could get us in, and he spoke to his friend Kelsey and they set up a private nighttime visit.

As we went through the White House, we could see into the Oval Office. A guard was positioned right outside the door, and some of the cleaning crew had been polishing the brass and the copper, making everything sparkle. We were able to observe where the President has his meetings.

As we were looking into the room, we could see a long table with the President's chair about an inch higher than anybody else's. Ronald Reagan was the President at this time, and the Marine on duty asked my granddaughter Jessica if she knew who the President was. If she had the right answer, she would get a prize. Well, Jessica had the answer right, so the Marine went into a drawer and pulled out a bag of jelly beans, which was Ronald Reagan's favorite candy. It was an awesome experience.

Billy did so much in his lifetime and I can imagine he was in pain every day of his existence. As his sister, he would confide in me at times how he was feeling. I'm sure he went to bed many nights with tears in his eyes because of ridicule, but he always found something else to be strong in and to start over in another venture.

When I turned sixty-five, my husband Wes was giving me a surprise birthday party with the help of my daughter Christine and her husband Michael. Billy was unable to attend because he was doing a show on stage in New York, so to let me know he was thinking of me, he wrote me a very sweet letter.

Photocopy of Billy's letter to Dede.
Letter courtesy of Dede Barty Morse

BILLY'S LETTER

October 6, 1991

Dear Dede:

We all knew that our act should have been Dede and the other two, but I must admit I had to pay Dad and our agent forty-five cents a week to keep the act known as Billy Barty and Sisters. One of the best moves Dad made was to give up show business so you and I could finish high school. Evelyn had already graduated from Hollywood High School and her major was fun! Today that class has been changed to drive-by shootings.

We were fortunate enough to go to Mar-Ken Professional School where we graduated in dating and jitterbugging. I went on to Los Angeles City College, and you continued your entertainment career.

The biggest problem you faced could be summed up in two words: "Judy Garland." You sang better and you acted better. The problem was, she married the owner of MGM and she could cry just saying hello.

The best move you ever made was when you married Wes. You have a great husband, family, step kids, your own kids, my wife Shirley and our family, and to top it off you still have Evelyn and me. Little Brother and Big Boss, we all love you!

But I tell you if you ever decide to do the act again, we will change our name to "Billy Barty and Friends."

We love you! Billy.

Billy studying.
Photo courtesy of Dede Barty Morse

A CALL FROM BILLY

Even though I would have liked to hear from Billy more frequently, I am always learning something new about him.

I remember a time I went to the doctor and confessed to him how I was feeling regarding Billy not calling me as often as I would have liked. The doctor and Billy had a common interest in horses, and so he went over to see Billy. As Billy and the doctor were talking, the doctor told Billy to go call his sister, and he jokingly handed Billy a dime. It wasn't long after that I received a call from my brother.

Billy had such an active schedule that it was amazing to me he could accomplish all that he was able to. I loved my brother dearly, but as with any family being so close, there were times we didn't like each other very much. For instance, I wanted him to slow down a bit as I felt he was working too hard. But Billy, being such a hard worker, didn't listen, and he tried to work until the end.

I remember the day before Billy passed away so vividly in my mind. It was in December of 2000 and Lori (my niece and Billy's daughter) had called me on the phone in tears, saying, "You better get down to the hospital, Aunt Dede, because Daddy is not going to be with us much longer."

The next morning I went down and picked up my niece Lori and we went to the hospital. Billy was in Intensive Care. I walked into the room, and while I was there, three specialists came in to observe one part of his body or another and he was not conscious. I introduced myself as Billy's sister and asked the question, "What exactly is going on?" Looking at Billy as I watched him on every kind of tube, I heard the doctor say, "There is very little hope."

All of Billy's systems were shutting down, and he never regained consciousness. I just sat there and I kissed him and said, "Thy will be done," and I left.

It was the next day that he died, December 23, 2000. A nurse walked into my brother's room and all the machines were turned off.

And then there was light....

The fireplace is singing its favorite song of warmth, and the candle that I have burning, *which is in the shape of a red rose,* is the symbol of love.

The increasingly brilliant candlelight is flickering all over the place, ever changing in direction and motion.

How understanding this flicker of light has been to all religious music this morning. The response is joyous to watch. There is so much to learn from watching the flame of a candle...

...and then there was light!

It is time to reflect on the past year and to do inventory of self to help us use the God-given qualities that are in us for good, ***and to say a very special thank you for all that we have.***

Barty family with Dede on the far right.
Photo courtesy of Dede Barty Morse

Ellen and Albert Barty by the car.
Photo courtesy of Dede Barty Morse

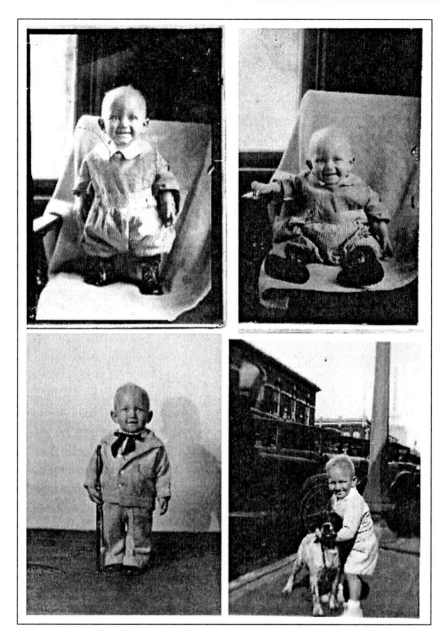

Baby Billy collage.
Photo courtesy of Dede Barty Morse

Young Billy in suit collage.
Photo courtesy of Dede Barty Morse

Billy cars and boat photo collage.
Photo courtesy of Dede Barty Morse

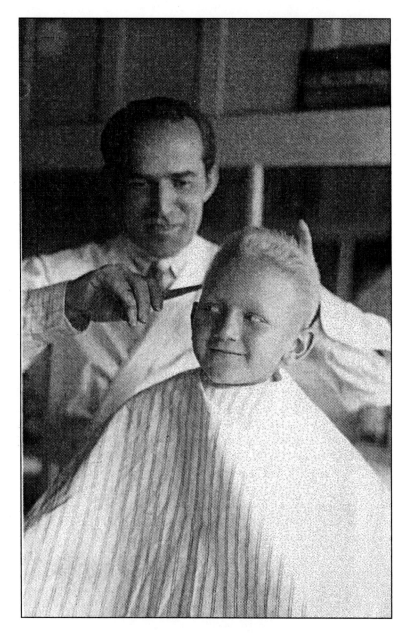

Billy getting a haircut.
Photo courtesy of Dede Barty Morse

Billy with accordian.
Photo courtesy of Dede Barty Morse

Billy and Evelyn Barty by the bench.
Photo courtesy of Dede Barty Morse

Albert and Ellen going to Dede and Wes's wedding.
Photo courtesy of Dede Barty Morse

Chapter Two

KROFFT PRODUCTIONS

Mark Evanier
Wendy Blair
Johnny Whitaker
John Philpott
Bill Ung

Mark Evanier, Johnny Whitaker, John Philpott, Bill Ung

MARK EVANIER
(Sid and Marty Krofft, writer, producer)

I was the head writer on a number of shows produced by Sid and Marty Krofft, and Billy was part of their stock company, cast in everything they did. I am 6'3", and often when I had to confer with Billy on some script point, I'd stoop or get down on one knee. We'd finish our discussion and he'd start to walk away. Then he would turn around, look at me still crouching in position, and grin, "I'm leaving now, you can get up!" One time we went to lunch together. Billy had all sorts of medical woes that made it difficult for him to walk, and since my parking space was on the other side of the lot, I said, "You wait here—I'll go get my car. "Don't bother," he said. Then he led me to this parking spot in a handicapped space, right outside where he was taping, and announced, "I'll drive." It was a big car—a Lincoln, I think. Bigger than any car that I ever owned. The front seat had been modified to bring it extra close to the dashboard and the gas pedal and brakes had extensions. Billy hopped effortlessly and comfortably onto a special, elevated cushion behind the wheel. I had no such ease trying to squeeze into the passenger spot. "You might be more comfy in the back," Billy chuckled, after watching me play twister for about two minutes. He was right. I was. And I recall hoping that someone I knew would see me being chauffeured around Hollywood by Billy Barty. One of the programs we did was a short-lived thing called the *Krofft Superstar Hour,* which comprised multiple segments. We did thirteen of them in "block scheduling," meaning that we taped thirteen openings, then thirteen closings, then thirteen episodes of a department called "Horror Hotel" and "Lost Island," though you would have never have known he was in the former. The Kroffts, as everyone knows, specialized in strange costumed creatures, and "Horror Hotel" was full of them.

The role that was assigned to Billy was that of Seymour the Spider, which involved a bulky, fur-covered costume that completely covered him. The character's voice was supplied by a wonderful actor named Walker Edmiston, who was situated at a nearby microphone. You couldn't see or hear Billy when he played

Seymour. There was no way anyone watching could have had any idea who was in the spider suit, but for the obvious fact that, whoever it was, he or she was pretty short. We began rehearsing, and the first time I watched Billy running madly around as Seymour, a little alarm bell went off in my noggin. Just being inside that get-up under hot lights was clearly an ordeal. Every break, when they took the headpiece off, he was drenched in perspiration, gasping for air—and he was not a young man. Worse, the role was very strenuous, involving a lot of chase sequences. Often it meant scurrying up and down stairs, and Billy had trouble walking, even out of costume. He was also having trouble seeing out of the eyeholes. I decided this wouldn't do and spent the rest of the afternoon chopping down Seymour's participation, assigning many of his lines and actions to others. This would not affect Billy's paycheck in any way. It just meant fewer hours in the spider suit, and less running, which I assumed would please him. It would conserve his strength for "Lost Island" in which he would appear without any identity-hiding costume, and where his acting skills were really needed. The next morning when I walked in, a production assistant ran up to me and said, "Thank God you're here! You're needed down on the set. It's Billy Barty!" "He hurt himself?" I asked, that was my first thought. "No, he's throwing a temper tantrum, saying he's going to quit or something. He demands to see you!" I ran down to the set, squatted next to a very irate Mr. Barty, and asked, "Billy, what's wrong?"

Furious, he waived the script revisions and yelled, "You cut me out of the show! I've been in show business for almost half a century, and nobody ever chopped my part down like this before!"

I started to quote the old maxim about there being no small roles, only small actors, then I thought better of it. What I actually said was, "Billy, we're trying to save your energy…" and he said, "You don't like my work?" "Billy, we love your work. You're irreplaceable and we need you healthy when we start taping 'Lost Island.' We just didn't want you to get hurt." "I'm an actor," he said again. "I'm being paid to act, just like everyone else here. I want to act!" "Okay," I shrugged. We went back to the old scripts and for the next two weeks, I watched Billy sweat and bump into things and become exhausted playing Seymour the Spider. And he loved every minute of it, because he was an actor and he was acting. At the same time we were doing the *Krofft* shows, Hervé Villechaize was playing Tattoo, the sidekick on *Fantasy Island*—you know, the diminutive guy with the thick accent who used to yell, "The Plane! The Plane!" Years later I wound up producing a special in which Mr. Villechaize appeared. He was a mean and troubled little man, and I mean "little" in both the physical and spiritual sense. He would grab and grope the women on the set. One woman in particular complained to the producer, which was me. Instead of rehearsing and learning his lines, he spent his time ordering around male employees and discomforting female ones. I mention all this to make a point of contrast: Hervé's *stardom,* such as it was, was based wholly on him being an oddity. That was why his career didn't last long. No one ever hired him because they thought he'd be good on camera. They just thought that he'd be short. Billy Barty was usually hired to be short, but also to be funny. That is why he was always in demand. He worked close to seventy years because he was an actor and loved acting.

He even loved it enough to run around for a few weeks in a stifling spider outfit with no one knowing who he was. But the story I want to close with occurred one day when we were doing the *Krofft Superstar Hour.* That week's *TV Guide* featured a cover story on Hervé that infuriated Billy.

He was stalking around our set, muttering unkind comments about Mr. Villechaize. I asked him why. His irritation, he explained, was because in the interview with *TV Guide,* Hervé insisted he was a midget, not a dwarf. Billy said that was a lie, and one that distressed him because he was working so hard to remove the negative implications of the word "dwarf." As he was explaining this to me, someone else came by and asked Billy what he was riled about. Billy answered them with what may be the funniest line I've heard uttered in thirty years, in and around show business. He said, "It's Hervé. He's passing for a midget!" I was squatting when he said it, and I fell over and just laughed for about twenty minutes. I'm laughing now, recalling his delivery. He really was a very funny man. I've been trying to figure out how to end this without some sort of "short" reference (you know, like, "He may have been 3'10", but he was a giant," blah, blah, blah). Too easy, too obvious. So I'll just say that Billy Barty was a great guy and a true professional. I'm very glad that he had a long, glorious career, because he certainly earned it.

WENDY BLAIR
Knave Productions *(The Smothers Brothers Show)*

I was the Production Supervisor on the series *Dr. Shrinker,* which starred Billy. *Dr. Shrinker* was a series produced by the Sid and Marty Krofft Company. It was part of the *Krofft Supershow,* which aired on Saturday mornings. We taped a bunch of them at KTLA, Channel 5 studios in 1975 or 1976. The show was about an island with a mad scientist (Billy was his loyal assistant) who shrank three teenagers down to about six inches. They were always escaping and facing dangers from bugs, spiders, and animals that were a hundred times their size. My recollection of Billy is that he was professional and nice to work with, and that he wasn't crazy about working with the monkey we had on one episode!

JOHNNY WHITAKER
(Family Affair, Tom Saywer, Sigmund and the Sea Monsters)

Ever since I can remember, I grew up in television, I grew up on television, and I grew up watching television. As a young boy coming home from work, I couldn't wait to see Billy Barty on his show. I always loved him because he was my size. All of the kids looked up to Billy—well, they looked at him, straight in the eye. Billy Barty was the person that every little kid wanted to meet.

Then I had the opportunity to meet him! Ever since that time and until today, I've been looking up to Billy Barty. I look up to him because he is the meaning of entertainment.

Sigmund and the Sea Monsters
Working with Billy for three years on *Sigmund and the Sea Monsters* and watching him getting in and out of the Sigmund costume was a chore in itself. But to watch Billy make that costume come to life, there was no other actor who could do so much as to what he had to do.

Work Ethics
The love that he showed me and the things that I learned from him were so great. He taught me the greatest things about comedy and timing and the importance of being a true entertainer. He taught me to work and to always be on the job and on time, no matter who you were, whether you were the star of the show or not, and how to make the producer happy. It was Billy Barty who has taught me those important things that I have never forgotten to this day.

JOHN PHILPOTT
("Courage" in *The Bugaloos*)

I often recall the time Billy and I shared together, "gig" talking. As well as being a respected actor, Billy was also a competent musician. Frequently we would sneak off during the shooting of *The Bugaloos* and go next door to Studio 20. Studio 20 was the second film set at Paramount Studios in Hollywood, and that is where he had his drum kit set up behind the scenes.

We would regularly take turns exchanging drum riffs and patterns. Sometimes we would be drumming for hours, that was, until we were missed. He was a self-taught drummer like me, and we had a lot in common. Preferring "live" music as I did, we would speak at length about our preferences and experiences and which British and American groups inspired us. I had the pleasure from playing on this drum set, which back then was the smallest drum kit in the world.

At that time I was still learning my profession and was very young, but at the same time Billy and I were having fun on and off the film set and having conversations about the film industry.

My memory of him is one of being very helpful, warm, friendly, and a person who liked a chat. He was an inspiration to us all!

BILL UNG
(*The Bugaloos* website)

I met Billy Barty at the Krofft Collectibles Auction in August 1998. He was a very warm and friendly man. He posed for some pictures, signed a few autographs, and got up to personally auction off the "Sparky" costume pieces from the Krofft Road Shows.

Although Billy was in his forties when he worked on *The Bugaloos*, nobody ever thought Sparky the Firefly was anything but a scared little kid, timid and shy, bumbling and foolish, heartwarming and sincere.

He fully personified the kid inside the costume, and produced a character that couldn't have been a better match for *The Bugaloos*.

Chapter Three

THE LITTLE PEOPLE OF AMERICA

*President George H.W. Bush
(Americans with Disabilities Act)
Supervisor Mike Antonovich
George Lucas
Paul Petersen
Buck Wolf
Leah Smith
Robert Van Etten
Angela Van Etten
Pat Lang
Danny Woodburn
Joe Martinez
James Giofreda
Shirley Pena
Robert Ahmanson*

President Bush and Billy collage
Photo courtesy of the Billy Barty Foundation

PRESIDENT GEORGE H.W. BUSH
The Americans with Disabilities Act

We will no longer underestimate the abilities of Americans with disabilities. We will treat Americans with disabilities as people to be respected, rather than problems to be confronted.

Some 43 million Americans have one or more physical or mental disabilities, and the number is increasing as the population as a whole is growing older. Historically, society has tended to isolate and segregate individuals with disabilities, including outright intentional exclusion. Census data, national polls, and other studies have documented that people with disabilities, as a group, occupy an inferior status in our society, and are severely disadvantaged socially, vocationally, economically, and educationally, which was the purpose of the passing of the Americans with Disabilities Act in 1990.

Information courtesy of the ADA.

Billy, Dede, and Mike Antonovich
Photo courtesy of Supervisor Mike Antonovich

SUPERVISOR MIKE ANTONOVICH
Los Angeles County

The Poet John Donne once called England "a little land with a huge heart." Something of the same thing could be said of Billy Barty, except for one aspect: don't let appearances fool you. There is nothing little about Billy Barty.

In the years that I've been privileged to call Billy a friend, we've often spoken together at schools and audiences of young people. I've always been impressed by his message that "the biggest obstacle anyone has to overcome is the space between their ears."

Supervisor Mike Antonovich
Photo courtesy of Mike Antonovich

Billy has been an inspiration to so many people, and not only as one of our finest actors; he also served as the former President Bush's Honorary Chairman for the "Access to Opportunity" program, and served as the Commissioner for the City of Los Angeles Commission on Disabilities.

He has given unsparingly of his time and wisdom to countless charities, and brightened the day of literally millions of children with disabilities. He has reminded these children, as he has reminded all of us, that there is no obstacle so large that it can't be overcome with a gigantic will, an open mind, and a huge heart.

He was never disabled. He was simply a good citizen who delivered help to those who needed help. He demonstrated this humanity and caring as my appointee on the Los Angeles County Commission on Disability.

He was a great talent, a great friend, and a great citizen!

Note of interest: Billy was godfather to Supervisor Mike Antonovich's son Michael.

Billy Barty is a man who has touched so many lives with entertainment and joy by caring and helping his fellow man. His achievements have certainly inspired all of us.

George Lucas Portrait
Photo courtesy of Billy Barty Foundation

Billy Barty

Born: Millsboro, Pennsylvania   October 25, 1924
Married to Shirley Barty   February 24, 1961

"Oh, We're Little People"

Oh, we're little people just you and I.
Just the same as any other gal or guy.
And this big country of the brave and free,
Was built by little people you and me.
The only difference I can see,
Between a millionaire and me,
Is that the million dollars
That he'd give to be
Just as happy as little people, you and me.

Oh it doesn't take a genius to punch a clock,
*   to push a plow to get things done.*
It takes a lot of little people to build a bridge,
*   to dig a ditch or carry a gun.*
Oh the good Lord loves us you can see because
*   he makes so many like you and me.*
Built this world and rested so that he'd be free
*   to keep on making little people like you and me.*

Interment at Forest Lawn, Glendale, California

Dedication of the Grave   *David Neilson*

"Oh, We're Little People" lyrics

CITY OF LOS ANGELES

IN TRIBUTE

THE LOS ANGELES CITY COUNCIL EXTENDS ITS
DEEPEST SYMPATHY TO YOU IN THE PASSING OF
YOUR LOVED ONE

BILLY BARTY

IN WHOSE MEMORY
ALL MEMBERS STOOD IN TRIBUTE AND REVERENCE
AS THE COUNCIL ADJOURNED ITS MEETING OF
JANUARY 3, 2001.

SINCERELY,

j. Michael Carey

J. MICHAEL CAREY, CITY CLERK

Presented by

COUNCILMEMBER MIKE HERNANDEZ

COUNCILMEMBER JOHN FERRARO

COUNCILMEMBER JOEL WACHS

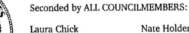

Seconded by ALL COUNCILMEMBERS:

Laura Chick	Nate Holden
Michael Feuer	Cindy Miscikowski
Ruth Galanter	Hal Bernson
Alex Padilla	Nick Pacheco
Mark Ridley-Thomas	Rudy Svorinich, Jr.
Rita Walters	

City of Los Angeles Memorial paper
Photo courtesy of Dede Barty Morse

Photo courtesy of Paul Petersen

PAUL PETERSEN
(Donna Reed Show)

A Minor Consideration

Dear friends, unless you have been a working kid actor, it would be difficult to explain the extraordinary lifetime relationships that have developed among child stars and the "little people." From the beginning, they have faithfully served as doubles, stand-ins, compatriots, and friends in the often cruel world of show business. The ties between kids and the "little people" flowed directly out of the circus world into the brand new world of Hollywood. From the time I started at age nine until I literally "out grew" my stand-in at age sixteen (platform shoes can be only so high), I was the beneficiary of the kind of friendship that, looking back, I see as priceless. Often it was just my co-worker and me against the full array of forces and personalities on the set. As a performer, I did not have to undertake risky stunts; in fact, whenever I considered doing a stunt, I was reminded that I was taking a little person's job. It seems odd to say this now, but there were many times when an overwhelming sense of loneliness enveloped me, and more often than not, I would be talking to Mimi (Shelly Fabares' stand-in) and Billy about the isolation I was feeling because of that peculiar thing called celebrity.

There will always be a special place in my heart for Billy Barty, as much for his friendship as for the leadership he provided his community. It's a matter of perspective, really, because the world appears different when you are small, and the professional company of "little people" that surrounds Hollywood has always made it their business to look after the kids.

BUCK WOLF
(ABC News)

I was truly a cub reporter when I met Billy Barty. It was in September 1988 and I was just beginning my education at the Columbia University School of Journalism.

Only two weeks into my program, I was given the daunting task of coming up with my master's project, which was a lengthy news feature on whatever subject I wanted to write about.

I was at a total loss for ideas. Thinking about all the journalism adages about how news writers should "stick up for the little guy" and "comfort the afflicted," I thought to myself, "Who are the real little guys?" That's how I decided to write about the everyday lives of little people, whom I then referred to, I'm sorry to say, as "midgets."

Two weeks later, I was in contact with the organization Little People of America, and my mentor on the project became Billy Barty. He was unbelievably generous with me being a student, giving of his time and insight. I spent large chunks of my school year with LPA members around New York.

I went to parties, LPA events, and private gatherings with little people. They shared with me their life experiences from simple things such as standing on a trash can to use an ATM machine, to facing their friends, co-workers, and even their families as little people.

The most important personal discovery I made in reporting my story on LPA was how hard it was for little people to join the organization. Many of them had led isolated lives, and others didn't want to associate with other little people. When I saw another little person for the first time, I recall an LPA-er tell me, "I said to myself, do I look like that? Do I walk funny like that guy? After listening to conversations going on two feet over my head for twenty years, I didn't know if I could handle speaking to someone else just like me—face to face. So when I saw another little person for the first time, I ran away. I was twenty at the time."

When I considered what LPA did for its members beginning in the late 1950's, I realized that it was in the forefront of America's group support systems, like Alcoholics Anonymous, and has done immeasurable good for this country.

My master's project, "Only Little On the Outside," won Columbia University's Wade Delores Science Writing Award in 1989. It was published as a Part Two cover story in *New York Newsday* in June of that year to coincide with Long Island New York's first regional LPA convention.

Billy Barty was unbelievably generous with me, and the sensitivity I learned in that project changed me personally and professionally.

Years later, when I worked for Court TV and ABC News, it served me very well.

Four years ago, reporting at the closing of the last leprosy center in the United States located in Carville, Louisiana, I felt as though I understood how it felt to deal with an illness that comes with a stigma that often hurts significantly more than the physical effects of the condition.

For the last three years I've covered entertainment for ABC News. I was given the assignment to write about *The Wizard of Oz* Munchkins' memories of Judy Garland. It was the last time I spoke with Mr. Barty, and once again, he was very kind with me.

Oz has always been considered a significant event in LPA history. It was the largest ever gathering of little people, and it helped inspire Barty to form LPA. But the filming of the movie also perpetuated some myths about little people. For years, the one hundred twenty-four little people who played the Munchkins had been fighting the perception that they ran amok during the filming of *The Wizard of Oz,* partaking in wild sex orgies and trashing their hotel.

Garland didn't help matters in the mid–1950's when talk-show host Jack Paar asked whether the Munchkins were little kids and she explained, "They were little drunks! They all got smashed every night." It was a hurtful remark, but the hatchet has long since been buried.

Munchkin Jerry Maren, who portrayed a member of "The Lollipop Guild," remembered Garland as a beautiful and kind young woman and an all-American teenager. "She was nothing but nice to us on the set," said the seventy-nine-year-old, four-foot five-inch actor, who went on to play Buster Brown in commercials and later served as a stand-in for Jerry Mathers on *Leave it to Beaver.*

"Judy used to bring candy to the set and give it out," said Margaret Pellegrini, a four-foot three-inch retired actress who played Sleepy Head. "She was just sixteen and she was a star, even then. But she was very friendly to us. Even if she made a negative remark, it doesn't change the way I feel."

"I had never been in a room full of people before when I didn't have to look up," Pellegrini said. Many marriages resulted from the film.

Some Munchkins complained that Hollywood treated them no better than animal acts. Show business impresario Leo "Papa" Singer acted as agent for most of the Munchkins and took a whopping fifty-percent commission.

Just to show you, in *The Wizard of Oz,* Ray Bolger, who played the Scarecrow, pulled in $5,000 a week. The Munchkins each took home $50.00 a week, and Toto the dog made $125.00 a week. "That's a lot of dog biscuits. Toto must have had a good agent," Maren joked. "That mutt should have been working for scraps."

Even though Billy didn't work on the film, he helped set the record straight. He said he knew Garland in the years leading up to her fatal overdose on sleeping pills in 1969. "She spoke fondly of working with the Munchkins," he said. "We were quite friendly, although I think she was a lonely person."

But why did she make that remark about the Munchkins being drunk all the time?

"Who knows?" Billy said. "Like a lot of things about Judy Garland, it is a mystery."

It was Billy's unique position as a celebrity and an advocate for little people that allowed him to do such things. He was a great man who made fantastic contributions to America. He will be missed, and we should all hope that other people of all sizes will help fill his role.

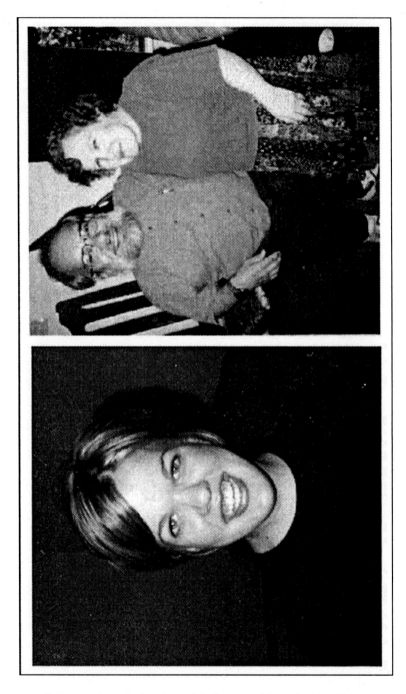

Collage of Leah Smith and Robert and Angela Van Etten.

LEAH SMITH
(Documentary, *Dwarf Standing Tall*)

As a little person, I know that Billy Barty was both an inspiration and a leader. His example taught me to just live my life—my way. He showed me that the only limits I have are the limits I put on myself. For little people as a group, he paved the way to come out of the shadows of self-doubt and stand our ground against ignorance and intolerance. By founding the Little People of America, he helped us develop a pride in our individuality and uniqueness. By developing this pride, we learned about the power, wisdom, and support we had as a team.

I will never forget the impact Billy's death had on me. I had flown all day, and upon arrival in New York City, I took a cab home. The cab driver broke the news to me about Billy's death. The disbelief and loss I felt must have shown on my face as I wondered about the future of LPA. I will never forget the cab driver's words. He said, "I don't know much about your organization, but I do know that Billy Barty really helped you out. Instead of feeling as if you lost your leader, just know that he successfully completed his job. Now it's time for someone else to take the stick and run with it." His words immediately changed my thinking. Billy brought us out of hiding, but now it's our turn to decide where we go from here. Billy Barty taught little people worldwide that it's not the size of your body that matters. It's the size of your heart that really counts.

For those of us who are of short stature, life presents a continuous parade of staring eyes. Doctors examine us with curiosity to see what they may have only read about in textbooks. The general public often views us as fairytale characters. In my own journey of understanding and identity, I have come to believe that I must be one of the true wonders of God's own creation. What has often been viewed as a curse or even just bad luck is truly a gift. There is only a small group of us that sees the world from this incredible view. Billy Barty helped us to focus our perspectives.

For me, this has also become my gift to the world. More than anything else, I hope that I can become part of what Billy started, and continue to educate people that "BIG" things do come in small packages.

ROBERT VAN ETTEN
(President, LPA South Florida Chapter)

I remember when I went to get married to my wife Angela in New Zealand that I had to depart through Los Angeles. I didn't realize in the morning that the plane wasn't going to leave until 11:00 p.m. that night, so I had a whole day to kill. I called up Billy and said, "Hey Billy, I'm in LA!" He picked me up at the airport, and we toured around and he showed me the spots.

When I first came in to the Little People of America back in 1976, I was in college and my first conference was in Miami Beach. Four years later, I ran for president of the organization. Billy was helping out the producers who were planning to do the movie *Under the Rainbow.* He was already a part of the acting crew, which didn't have total control on the actual script. But they had approached LPA, and I remember Billy doing the introduction for them. Their approach was to do a "documentary" about what really happened behind the scenes in the making of *The Wizard of Oz.* Of course, we didn't know who was going to be in it, except we had an indication that Billy already had some major part. We said, "Oh, fine—this is great," but we learned later as they were actually doing auditions, and people read parts of the script, some of the members came back and said, "Is this really going to be a documentary? There are some really crazy scenes in there." So here I was just elected President of the LPA. I had to investigate this whole thing and found out that maybe his film wasn't going to be a true documentary after all. When I asked the producer for the script, we realized then that it was going to be a slapstick comedy. We noticed they were stretching the history, and we later learned that Chevy Chase was going to be in the movie. We knew Billy was going to have a major role, but we had to tell the members that what was relayed to us, about this being a documentary, wasn't the case.

We sent letters out to all the members explaining that it was to be a slapstick comedy. Many members were upset. In the letter, we were not telling them that they couldn't participate in the film, but that it was up to them, and that the LPA could not endorse the film. Billy was upset about that, but in the end he did understand. When the movie came out, it did get good reviews from the critics, and some of our members who did participate enjoyed the experience.

I remember another time at one of our conferences that a film crew wanted to do a segment on the synthetic human growth hormone. It was supposed to be a documentary, and we had to tell them that their viewpoint wasn't correct. They thought giving this human growth hormone to our members would make them all grow taller, and they hadn't understood the concept that this hormone would help only a very small minority of our members.

So Billy had this special knack of being able to work with the media on the public relations side. But it was kind of a learning curve to us. Billy would tell us what angle to go on if we wanted the press to proceed along with it, and also what to do to hold them off. He was always there to give advice. Many members learned through him more about participating in his golf tournaments. He always had top entertainers at his golf tournaments and showed how a good celebrity event could be pulled off.

Billy had struggles between the Foundation and his many acting roles; therefore, he had to entrust other volunteers of the Billy Barty Foundation to other people to do a lot of the work. Sometimes these people did a marvelous job and sometimes they didn't. You might not have seen it the year it all happened, but it would show up a year or two later when you looked closer at the financial books.

Every time Billy would come to the LPA conferences, people would be lining up just to shake his hand. They would say to themselves, "I met a star. I met Billy!"

And it was important for the organization to have Billy out in the public eye. He had his way of approaching things from the entertainment side.

Unfortunately, the LPA was going through a growth period in which we were encouraging our members not to go in the entertainment world but rather into the professional world. There was always a little bit of resistance by which direction Billy was going in and which direction we were going in. Something that I have always learned is that you have to accept both. A number of little people, just like the general population, aren't going to go to college and will never be students, so the entertainment side may be more suitable for them. And if that's where they feel they can be challenged, be successful, and bring in enough income to raise a family, then why not? We do get a little bit critical as to what roles they play, as you are seeing right now with "dwarf tossing." A person may be able to make $500.00 a night, but what kind of image is he creating? We tell our members that if they are going to go into acting, they should diversify themselves in roles that other people can play, not just little people in typecast roles. Unfortunately, Billy came from that generation in which little people were typecast, but he had to make a living out of it and that is what he did. As I saw in the earlier pieces that Billy did, he was brilliant in putting together some of the comedy acts in those earlier shows of vaudeville days, and he carries that earlier history today.

Dwarf Collage
Photo courtesy of the Billy Barty Foundation

ANGELA VAN ETTEN
(Author, *Dwarfs Don't Live in Doll Houses*)

After we did the show on Sally Jesse Raphael in 1989, Billy contacted us and was very pleased that I and a young college student named Heidi Heinrich (a political science major) had talked against "dwarf tossing." He said that he was proud of us and that we represented LPA (Little People of America). He thought we did a really good job at speaking out against it, and encouraged us to keep going. Dwarf tossing has been banned in Florida since 1989, and there has been no activity since then until Mr. Flood came along recently, trying to have that ban overturned.

My husband Robert was the national president twice for the LPA. One time Billy was coming through town and stayed with us a night when we were living in Cleveland. When he came it was winter and he didn't have a coat, so he borrowed one of my husband's.

The first time I met Billy it was the twenty-fifth anniversary of the LPA, and the conference was in Reno. I noticed that Billy would always take time for people, especially to have his picture taken with children.

He used to always sit in on the board meetings of the LPA, even when he was not on the board, and took an interest in what was happening.

There was some controversy about Billy being the only founder of the LPA and when it came out Robert, my husband, was the president.

Billy had written a book, and some of the original members were upset with him. As with any organization, there was a core group of people who were there when it began. Somehow their names got lost in the shuffle, and because Billy was a celebrity, his name rose to the top and he was the one listed as the founder.

It is a shame that there had to be a controversy because they needed each other. They needed Billy because he pulled in the media and had people all over the country knowing about the organization.

In view of the fact that Billy was more of a "visionary" and active in Hollywood, he needed a core group of people to do the everyday business of the organization. He would lend his name to things, and was a really great guy. Some people thought that he was trying to get his name out in the public view to advance his own career, but I don't think that myself. If you look at his life, he was still involved even if there was no gain in it at all for him.

You have to wonder if Billy had been born into a different generation what he would have been able to do. He accomplished so much with so few resources.

Angela Van Etten is not only the author of the book *Dwarfs Don't Live in Doll Houses,* but she also has a law degree and can practice in New York and Ohio.

Lang family collage
Photos courtesy of Pat Lang

PAT LANG
(Treasurer, LPA South Florida Chapter)

I became a member of the LPA (which is where I knew Billy) in 1972, and Reno was my first convention. My husband and I were part of the first ten charter members in Florida started by Bill Albaugh. Bill Albaugh was also in show business, and we learned a lot about Billy Barty through him. I was president of the local chapter in Florida for four years, treasurer for thirteen, and now I am writing a newsletter. My husband Ed was also president locally, and then became editor for the newsletter nationally, which was another four years. Ed used to work about thirty to forty hours on the newsletter because he had to keep in touch with people all over the country.

Billy helped many people get to conventions who couldn't have gone otherwise. There was a fund that was set up especially for first-time visitors, and he would give them a stipend toward airline tickets or whatever was needed. The money that comes in for the LPA is put into different funds for scholarships and special medical assistance. Recently we had two families who needed to go to Johns Hopkins and couldn't afford to fly up there, so we paid airfare for both families. Surgery for a little person is not a one-time trip and can be very expensive. There are no salaries at the LPA, and every job is on a volunteer basis. We want to take whatever money we get to help out other little people.

When we attended the conventions, we tried to be around Billy, even if it was just to listen. So many people were coming up to him, wanting his attention as well. At the time I first started going to the LPA conventions, there were only a few hundred people. LPA now has several thousand members worldwide, and about fifteen to sixteen hundred people make it to the conventions. I became more involved when I went to the convention in North Carolina. I participated in the fashion show, and I made my own clothes. They have so many things going on in these conventions.

My daughter Dawn was also in the fashion show, and my son David was in the talent segment because he could play the trumpet. We would spend a lot of time meeting people and talking because in your own location, you are limited where you live, as to how many little people you are going to meet. The socialization of being with other little people was super because everyone had a similarity as to where they fit in. Even though there may have been other core people at the beginning of the LPA, Billy was most accepted as the founder. I really think he had the majority of the effort behind making it happen. He was a dynamic person and would always get things together.

DANNY WOODBURN

A tribute to Billy Barty for his memorial
Courtesy of Dede Barty Morse

I will always remember Billy as a friend to me even before I knew who he was.

He did many great things for me directly and indirectly, whether it was in thinking of me for an event or a job, supporting me like a fan in my work as I was of his, working to eliminate the evil and hateful language used to describe "little people" even before I was born, or clearing a path through prejudice and then paving the road.

The last time I saw Billy was at the "Battle of the Batons" where he passed the baton to me while conducting the LA Junior Philharmonic. I can only hope I can carry that baton and conduct myself the same way he did.

JOE MARTINEZ
On the serious side

My name is Joe Martinez and I am also an LP actor. About twelve years ago in 1990, there was an unfortunate incident that happened to another LP actor by the name of David·Rappaport. He was in *Time Bandits,* and was a friend of Billy Barty.

Well, to my sadness, he ended his life. At that time, he was becoming a somewhat regular on *LA Law.* There was a lot of speculation as to why he committed suicide. I was tired of all the speculating as to why he did it and thought it was more proper to recognize the body of work that he did. So I wrote an article with an illustration about it in the LPA *Mini Gator Gazette.* This reached Billy Barty. He saw it and read it, and really liked the article. He ended up writing a letter back to me that was forwarded on to me through the *Gazette.* I still have the letter with me. It is personally signed by him, and I have kept it all these years. This letter was written on May 14, 1990, a couple of weeks after the death of David Rappaport.

The letter reads:
Dear Mr. Martinez,

I just read your text and saw your illustration in regards to a friend of mine, Mr. David Rappaport in the *Mini Gator Gazette.* May I congratulate you, not only on the content, but also on your approach to a very sensitive subject. I had the pleasure of working with David in an educational film six years ago called *Stone Mountain* in Atlanta, Georgia. We also went out several times and he was a delight.

As you commented, I too do not have an answer, nor do I want to speculate as some newspapers and individuals have. I've had many calls from the wire services, radio, and TV stations wanting my thoughts regarding this unfortunate incident. My reply was no reply. Thank you for your comments, Mr. Martinez, and I hope other LP's will follow your remarks.

Sincerely, Billy Barty

JAMES GIOFREDA

I had the honor of meeting Billy at the Little People of America convention in Boston, Massachusetts, in 1983. I am a little person with Achondroplasia, and Boston was my first convention. I was twelve years old at that time and had seen Billy in the movie *Under the Rainbow* and some television specials.

I was so excited to meet him, and when we did meet, he made me feel as if we had been friends forever. Of the many years I went to the conventions, that was the feeling I always had from him. He would put out his hand and say, "Hey there, Tiger" and made me feel welcome.

Sally Jesse Raphael

I had the privilege of joining him on the Sally Jesse Raphael talk show on "little people." We had a great time.

In my opinion, Billy was one of the bravest men I ever knew. What he did for little people and people with disabilities was absolutely phenomenal. Getting together with twenty other people and forming a nation-hood is amazing. I have him to thank for creating the Little People of America organization, which has been so good to me. I met my beautiful wife, who also has Achondroplasia, through that organization and have met many life-long friends.

My wife and I have a wonderful three-year-old son who has our condition. I only wish he could have had the chance to meet this great man. He will be missed dearly and will always live in our hearts.

SHIRLEY PENA
(A fan)

Years ago, my sister was considering joining Mr. Barty's organization for small people and she wrote for information. She was barely above height requirement to qualify. However, Mr. Barty was very gracious in his reply to her letter, giving her much encouragement in her life choices. He was genuine and understanding in listening to her childhood "horror stories."

Suspended from the high hook
One time during her high school years, older male students actually suspended her from the high hook of a hall closet, where she remained until finally being freed by a horrified teacher who found her hours later.

ROBERT AHMANSON
(Ahmanson Foundation)

When I came out from Omaha, Nebraska, I was seventeen years old and a bit frightened at that time. Evelyn Barty ended up working for my uncle, Howard Ahmanson, for over thirty years. I used to go over to the Barty house and get together with Billy, Evelyn, and Dede. Ellen Barty (Billy, Dede, and Evelyn's mom) always had a pot of minestrone soup on the stove.

He Never Acted Small
One thing I noticed about Billy is he never acted small. When you met him the first time, you would say, gee he's small. And then when you met him the second time, you wouldn't see his size. He was just Billy Barty.

I spent my first New Year's Eve at the Barty house with Billy and Dede, but one of my fondest memories is when we would all go out to a particular restaurant on Saturdays because they were having "short ribs."

People would come up to Billy in the restaurant and say, "Oh, you're Billy Barty!" Then he would get up and go around to the tables and meet the people.

Life as a Little Person
One of the main things Billy wanted to do was make things easier to grasp for little people. We worked on it together, and we lowered the height of the light switches in his house but ran into problems with the city codes. Eventually the codes were changed. We worked on other projects as well, using drawers at the bottom of cabinets as little stepladders to help him reach things.

He was determined to make life easier for people of short stature, and was one of the most dynamic people I have ever met.

*Photo collage of Evelyn Barty with her birthday cake and
Thanksgiving with Albert and Ellen and Billy Barty.
photos courtesy of Dede Barty Morse*

Chapter Four

LITTLE HOUSE ON THE PRAIRIE

Anecdote from Billy
"Little Lou" synopsis
Kent McCray
Susan Sukman McCray
Stan Ivar
Allison Balson
Kevin Hagen
Ken Berry
Patrick Loubatiere

ANECDOTE FROM BILLY
"The Phone"

"I went to make a phone call. I'm bold and not afraid to ask someone to put a coin in the telephone for me. I can reach the receiver but I can't reach the coin box."

The operator said, "Please deposit another thirty-five cents."

I said, "I can't."

She said, "What did you say?"

I said, "I can't deposit the money because I am only 3'9" tall and I can't reach the coin box."

Then, there was silence.

She said, "Are you Billy Barty?"

I said, "Yes, I'm on the telephone, not on the television. How did you know that I was Billy Barty?"

She said, "I watched you last night on a rerun of a *Little House on the Prairie* episode, and I recognized your voice."

I said, "What do you want me to do?"

She said, "Hang up!"

"LITTLE LOU" SYNOPSIS
starring Billy Barty

There was an episode of *Little House on the Prairie* that Billy starred in called "Little Lou." Watching him fight the stigma of being a circus performer and the physical hardship that he obviously endured during this episode was very heart wrenching. Because it is a sample of what little people endure on a daily basis, it should put many of our everyday woes in the proper perspective.

In this particular episode, Lou's wife (Patty Maloney) died after giving birth to their baby girl Cynthia. Lou (played by Billy) now had to find a job in town to support his family. Being rejected because of his height by Harriet Oleson (Katherine McGreggor), he was prevented from finding work. He ended up stealing at Oleson's store to provide for his family. Harriet Oleson was suspicious that Lou Bates was the culprit of this crime, and had no mercy on him when he was confronted. Wanting to press charges against him, she had her husband Nels (Richard Bull) put him in the icehouse until the authorities came. While he was there, Harriet and Nels' daughter Nancy (Allison Balson) fell into a dry well. Lou was the only person small enough to pull her out of the well. No matter how awfully he had been treated by Mrs. Oleson, he was quick to respond, and Nancy was freed. At the end of the show, Harriet apologized profusely to Lou Bates, and he told her that he forgave her and *that he isn't a small man.*

KENT McCRAY

(Producer of *Bonanza, Highway to Heaven, Little House on the Prairie*)

The first time I met Billy was on a Bob Hope Show in the late fifties.

One thing about Billy is that when he came to work, he came prepared. He was always there, and you never had to find him. He was a professional from the word go.

Michael Landon and Billy did a lot of charity work together. Michael remarked many times that Billy's caring for people always came through in his work and through his personal life.

If Michael Landon or Victor French were here, I am sure they would have a few stories to tell.

Billy and Victor French were actually neighbors. I think they lived about three doors down from each other.

All through *Little House* and *Highway to Heaven,* Victor was with us and would often talk to Billy in the yard. Then when Victor would come in late, he would say he was down helping Billy Barty doing a few things (instead of just talking to Billy).

I said, "I bet you were!"

As soon as we read a story line in the episode "Little Lou," we automatically thought about Billy with his professionalism and how he reacted to things.

SUSAN SUKMAN MCCRAY

(Casting director for *Little House on the Prairie* and *Highway to Heaven*)

The Episode "Little Lou"

Little House: A New Beginning

That particular episode was the first year I had cast Stan Ivar in the show as a regular. It was also the first year that Michael Landon decided he wanted to just direct some and write some, and didn't want to be a regular in the cast every week. So we had to find a new family to move into the "Little House." This was the first role that Stan had a major role, and it was very special to him. (He and Billy were the stars of the episode "Little Lou.") Every show on *Little House* was a bit of a challenge, because Michael Landon always came up with something that would tug at someone's heart. Invariably it would be someone who was out of the "norm" or someone who was ill, or someone who had a terrible problem to overcome, and of course the Kleenex would come out like crazy.

Family TV

We accomplished a lot by doing those stories and had incredible results. Today you don't find anyone open to listening to ideas like the ones that Michael had. My husband Kent McCray was Michael Landon's partner and producer for many years, and unfortunately today the powers that be along with the networks don't understand those types of shows. They just don't feel that they will have an audience, so it is almost impossible to approach them.

I wish Michael Landon were still alive. He adored Billy. They had a lot of fun together, and he enjoyed having Billy on the show with us in the "Little Lou" episode.

A Dramatic Role

It was a great experience for Billy to do the "Little Lou" episode because he really enjoyed having a nice dramatic role to play, and it certainly was a special role for him.

He was a very loving, sweet, kind man, and once people met him and got to know him and talk to him, they didn't see any difference in his size from what we call the norm. It was totally overlooked because of *the man*. He had quite a career and knew a lot of people.

Billy Barty, Dean Butler, and Stan Ivar.
Photo courtesy of Stan Ivar

STAN IVAR

(John, *Little House on the Prairie*)

"A New Beginning"

Billy and I worked together on the TV show *Little House: A New Beginning* in an episode called "Little Lou." That particular episode was my introduction into the first television show that I had worked. I was one of the new actors there, and Billy and I used to joke a bit. "I am 6'1", not too tall but not too short." Anyway, while Victor French was directing, he said he wanted to get a two-shot of me and Billy. Needless to say, Billy made a joke regarding the difference in our sizes. He was a great guy and I had a wonderful time with him.

Photo courtesy of Stan Ivar

Stan Ivar

Pat Roylance, Melissa Gilbert, Michael Landon, and Stan Ivar.
Photo courtesy of Stan Ivar

Little House cast photo
Photo courtesy of Stan Ivar

ALLISON BALSON
(Nancy on *Little House on the Prairie*)

I have been reflecting upon my memories of Billy Barty and have realized my admiration for him, both as an actor and a person.

As an actor, Billy represented professionalism. As a person, Billy embodied goodness.

I met Billy when he guest starred on the episode "Little Lou" on *Little House on the Prairie*. This provided me a fortunate opportunity to work on several scenes directly with him. He was one of my favorites to work with because he was a truly dedicated actor. His energy and spirit were refreshing and uplifting.

This particular shoot that we did together challenged Billy physically and mentally. My character, Nancy Oleson, had fallen into a dry well and was trapped. Billy's character was my one hope for rescue. He was the only person in town with the physical proportions and strength required to bring me out by being lowered into the well himself.

Even with the obvious physical and mental strain of such an intense scene, Billy shined brightly. He did not let the difficulties of the shoot distract him. I believe he would have done that scene a hundred times if asked, because he himself was a perfectionist with a smile.

Billy Barty was a great man, with a heart of pure kindness. I remember him with fondness and great admiration.

Allison and Billy.
Photo courtesy of Bernice Balson

KEVIN HAGEN

Kevin Hagen.
Photo courtesy of Kevin Hagen

KEVIN HAGEN

(Doc Baker, *Little House on the Prairie*)

I loved Billy and have great admiration and respect for him. Billy was the star of the best of the *Little House* episodes that included me, and I loved spending those days with him.

I enjoyed his friendship when I played in his "Little People" golf tournament most every year.

We played and laughed away the days and nights. He is and will always be one of my most favorite people—big or little.

Little House collage: Allison Balson, Ken Berry, Patrick Loubatiere
Photo courtesy of Bernice Balson, Ken Berry, Patrick Loubatiere

KEN BERRY
(Mayberry RFD, Mama's Family)

I've known Billy Barty for a long time, and I would run into him in Studio City and the Moorpark Pharmacy in Studio City, California. Although I can't remember any specific incident with Billy, he was always a pleasure to see and I liked him very much. My niece went to school with Billy's daughter Lori, and from time to time she would go over to their house and then tell me about it.

Little House on the Prairie
"Annabelle"

Ken Berry played in an episode of *Little House on the Prairie* called "Annabelle" with Billy Barty, which aired October 15, 1979. His part was twofold. Not only did he play a clown, but he was also owner of the circus called "London's Circus."

The star of the show was Harriet Gibson, who played Annabelle. The program was centered on her obesity and on Billy, playing her friend Owen, who was all of 3'9" tall. Nels (played by Richard Bull) found when the circus came to town that the oversized woman was his sister Annabelle. Embarrassed because of her size, he ignored her and acted as though he never had seen her before. Annabelle was hurt and told the circus performers about the situation. They all surrounded her, and Owen (Billy Barty), in her defense, suggested that they leave town instead of performing.

Needless to say, Annabelle was ridiculed, mocked, and rejected because she was overweight. But those that traveled with her in the circus loved her and rallied around because they accepted her for who she was. In Billy's own life, he too has fought the discrimination of others because of his size. He had spent many years proving to others that size isn't what makes a person. It is what is in your heart that counts.

PATRICK LOUBATIERE

(Writer of the first book ever written about the *Little House on the Prairie* TV show, in any language: *La Petite Maison dans la Prairie-Walnut Grove: Terre Promise* (1999)).

Although we don't get every American movie and television series in France, everybody here knows Billy Barty—if not by name, at least by face. When it comes to famous dwarf actors, people often remember the one who was on *The Wild West,* the one who was on *Fantasy Island,* and Billy Barty, the one who is everywhere else! Indeed, Billy Barty's omnipresence on screen is absolutely phenomenal. I personally watched Billy for the first time in the seventies as a guest star of such TV series as *The Man from Atlantis, The Love Boat,* and *CHiPs.* I was a child at that time and, of course, I didn't know anything about Billy's glorious past. I was just happy to see, every now and then, this actor on my television who radiated kindness and who could move me as often as he made me laugh. Then, growing up, I found out who the real Billy Barty was. I realized the incredible length of his film career (seventy years) and of course his dedication to other little people. So, when I started writing my book about *Little House on the Prairie,* I wanted to highlight Billy. Although he played in only two episodes of the series, I wrote twenty lines about him, and included a small photo as well, which was more than I did for any other guest star. As was the case of most of the shows on which he worked, Billy left his mark on *Little House.* He first appeared on the 1979 episode "Annabelle" as a member of a circus troupe conducted by popular sitcom actor Ken Berry. Ken told me in an interview how much he enjoyed working with Billy. But Billy was especially memorable in the episode "Little Lou."

How can anyone forget his moving interpretation of Lou Bates, whose wife had died after giving birth, and who must face the attacks of Mrs. Oleson, who refuses to see someone "different" settling down in her community? What people usually don't know about this episode is that it played an important part in the future of *Little House.* At the time—autumn 1982—the show was undergoing a radical transformation. Michael Landon had begun an off-camera role, and even the title had changed to *Little House: A New Beginning*! Aware that these major changes would disgruntle a good number of the series' fans, Michael needed intense stories. He took one of the very first scripts he had written for *Bonanza* in 1969, "It's a Small World," and re-adapted it to *Little House*. Billy was chosen to play the lead, replacing Michael Dunn in the *Bonanza* version, and Patty Maloney, a favorite co-star of Billy's, played his wife. Michael had done several similar adaptations, with varying degrees of success, but this one was of his best efforts, mainly thanks to Billy.

Chapter Five

THE WALTONS

Judy Norton
Earl Hamner

JUDY NORTON
(Mary Ellen, *The Waltons*)

I was very inspired by knowing and having the honor to work with Billy Barty. He was a true legend, the kind of person who gave to others through his work and joy of living. Always quick with a smile, he never made me feel insignificant because I was "just a kid."

When Billy worked on the episode "The Carnival" on *The Waltons,* he was professional, and yet fun to be with. This was an episode about circus performers, and I remember numerous takes as we attempted to get the stunt sequences. I never once heard Billy complain or felt he was impatient with the endless repetition.

A truly "Big Spirit"
After *The Waltons,* I had the opportunity to participate in charity golf tournaments with Billy that bore his name. I was flattered that he always remembered me whenever our paths crossed. I thought this showed great class and reflected his genuine interest in people. This was proven by his generosity in lending his name and support to charity events so that he could help others. I was saddened to hear of his passing, but know that he will always be remembered as a truly "big spirit."

Judy Norton.
Photo courtesy of Judy Norton

Earl Hamner.

EARL HAMNER
(Writer, *The Waltons*)

I first met Billy on *The Waltons* and thought he did a wonderful job. He was a thorough pro on the set and knew a good many people there because he had done so much work in film and television.

He had a very endearing quality with people and carried himself with great dignity and poise. Billy was friendly and cordial to everyone.

After he worked on the television series, I ran into him often because we both went to the same pharmacy, called the Moorpark Pharmacy. Al, the owner, had built a special shelf marked the "Billy Barty Shelf" for him. He would leave packages for Billy there. The special thing about that shelf was that it was within Billy's reach.

What a sweet guy. How nice to have been associated with him.

Chapter Six

MOVIES

George Lucas
Willow
Tom Cruise
Lew Hunter
A.C. Lyles
Special Moments in Entertainment
Al Yankovic

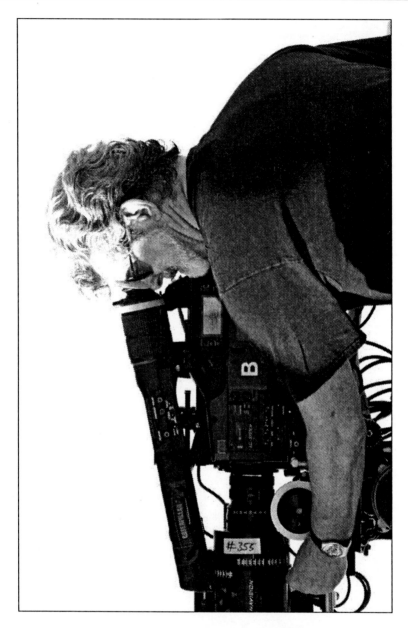

George Lucas on the set of Star Wars.
Photo courtesy of George Lucas

GEORGE LUCAS
(Lucas Films)

I first met Billy when we were working on *Willow*. I obviously was familiar with his work and had always been impressed with his characterizations and the exuberance he brought to the roles.

His part in *Willow* was that of a well-respected leader in the Village. Those qualities fit Billy to a "T."

He was always very jovial and fun and he loved to get into conversations. We'd sit and talk on the set quite a bit. He had a lot of opinions, and I always enjoyed the time we spent together.

I think Billy will be remembered for his tremendous contribution to the film industry and for the memorable characters he created bringing strength to every character he played.

WILLOW
One of Billy's favorite movies to do was *Willow*. He described it as being a very happy set, with the exception of bad weather. He said it was wet and damp all the time, and they were shooting out in the mud on an estate outside of London. His concern was that he didn't want any little person to have to walk in the mud. He wanted them all to be driven around and taken care of.

When Lucas Films was casting for little people in *Willow*, they issued a casting call all across England. They were able to hire sixty-five people, but they needed two hundred twenty-five. So the casting call went out all across Europe.

The end result was that they had a cast that spoke thirteen different languages, all trying to work together on the set. When it was time to depart, they were all hugging, kissing, and crying because no one wanted to see each other leave.

In *Willow*, everyone had a wonderful time. The most important thing to Billy was the fact that people were used as human beings. They had love interests, family interests, and concerns, all very human, only small.

(*Willow Magazine*, Bill Warren)

Tom Cruise (Legend)
Photo courtesy of Tom Cruise

TOM CRUISE

Early on in my career, I had the great honor and sincere pleasure of working with Billy Barty on a film called *Legend*.

The first time I met him, I was struck with the realization that this was Mustard-Seed, Billy's character from the 1935 version of William Dieterle and Max Reinhardt's *A Midsummer Night's Dream*, and thought, "My God, he's truly a legend!"

Billy's enthusiasm and professionalism for his work and his undying dedication to helping others were an inspiration.

LEW HUNTER
(NBC)

I was so fond of Billy. He used to come in my NBC office when I was director of development. He would always leave me with joy in my heart, a smile on my face, and a "Thank you, God, for Billy Barty" thought in my soul.

Maybe four or five times he would come to my office to sell me a series or movie. I first saw him on stage in the Stuart Theatre in Lincoln with Spike Jones in 1952. Great show, great man.

A.C. Lyles.
Photo courtesy of A.C. Lyles

A.C. LYLES
(Paramount)

I remember we had a dinner for Ronald Reagan and we had a lot of celebrities there. Rosey Grier, who was a towering football star, probably six foot four and two hundred fifty pounds, was standing on the stage talking. Suddenly his legs were pulled apart, and Billy emerged from between his legs. As you can imagine, there was little Billy and this big mammoth of a man, looking out to the audience and saying, "My name is Billy Barty. I almost grew up in Hollywood!"

Billy had this magnificent vision. Although he was small, he could see everyone who came into the room. When he saw people that he knew and people that he loved, he was like a little puppy dog with so much enthusiasm and personality. He was constantly driving to help other people.

At his funeral, it was remarkable to see the turnout of those in various positions in the motion picture entertainment business.

There were writers, directors, producers, stars, cameramen, art directors, prop men, grip men, electricians, stand-ins, and makeup people. He had a tremendous coverage of individuals there.

He by no means ever lost his obsession with the entertainment business, but he had as much zeal for his quest for the little people. I've never known anyone to be more devoted to that organization than he was.

At Billy's memorial there were so many little people gathered in one place to honor their hero.

You can almost talk to anyone in our business and mention the last name Barty, and they will know that it is Billy. That's a legend. He was a delightful, wonderful human being who pleased his friends and a wide audience.

Some people were born to be entertainers, and Billy Barty was one of those people. He was so clever and so wonderful over the years.

SPECIAL MOMENTS IN ENTERTAINMENT
Memories from Billy

The Wizard of Oz

After college, my dream was not to return to acting, but rather to be a sportswriter or a sportscaster. But one day in 1946, my friend Jerry Maren, the "Lollipop Kid" in *The Wizard of Oz,* said, "Come on, Billy, let's go over to Metro and audition for *Three Wise Fools*" (1946). We were both hired for the film, and I was off to follow the Hollywood road again. At age fourteen, I was too young to get a part at MGM's *The Wizard of Oz* (1939), which employed one hundred twenty-five little people (more than any film until *Willow,* which employed three hundred). By law, you had to be eighteen to work the long hours that the film demanded. In many films, I was cast as the "mischievous child," and I appeared in baby roles until I was almost eight. I then played eight-year-olds for five years, which is one rare advantage to being a little person actor. One disadvantage is that a little person is not likely to be cast as a leading man.

Foul Play

I am forever indebted to a special effects person on the *Foul Play* set (1978) who forgot to score a vase (to make it break easily). Goldie Hawn was supposed to hit me over the head. First strike, it didn't break. Goldie struck it again; it didn't break. Finally on the third blow, the vase began to crumble. Talk about seeing stars! Goldie was so upset that for the next half-hour, she held me on her lap and applied ice to my forehead. Despite the pain, I found myself transported back to the time when "America's Sweetheart," Mary Pickford, had held me on her lap after my appearance with the Hollywood Baby Orchestra at *Pickfair.*

The Day of the Locust

When I was handed the script for *The Day of the Locust* (1975), a chilling story about Hollywood in the 1930's, I was shocked by some of the language in the script. Here was an opportunity to work with the highly regarded director John Schlessinger, but for me, to use profanity, even in a film, posed a moral issue.

At the reading, I was offered the role. I explained to Mr. Schlessinger and to the producer, Jerome Hellman, that I would have a difficult time with some of the dialogue. They generously offered to let me change any words that bothered me as long as it didn't interfere with the role of the story line.

It remains one of my favorite film roles because it took me out of comedy and allowed me to be recognized as a dramatic actor.

I did all my own stunts in *Locust*.

Mickey McGuire Comedy Shorts

Early on in my career I worked in dozens of the "Mickey McGuire" comedy shorts that starred my friend Mickey Rooney. All of us kids did many stunts that child actors would not be allowed to do today. I remember having to shimmy down the side of a building on a rope for one scene, and for another, swinging like Tarzan from rooftop to rooftop.

Al Yankovic

AL YANKOVIC
(UHF)

Near the end of his career, Billy was sensitive about taking roles that were specifically written for little people. I was very thankful when he agreed to play TV news cameraman Noodles MacIntosh in my 1989 movie *UHF.*

The running gag was that every single one of Noodles' shots was taken at extreme low angles. That's a joke that just wouldn't have played if we'd had to cast Jamie Farr or something. We gave Billy a single card credit on the opening titles even though he had a small part. Contractually we weren't obligated to do so, but we did so because we were happy to have him in the film.

I wish I had spent more time with him on the set. About all I really remember is that he was a total pro, and he was loved by everybody. I also think he was fond of carrot sticks at the service table.

Chapter Seven

ENTERTAINERS/TV/FILM

Walter Winchell

Peter Marshall

Pat Boone

Jack Narz

David Narz

Mickey Rooney

Jan Rooney

Dick Clark

Tom Bosley

Pat Morita

Don Knotts

Ed Asner

Betty White

Dick Van Patten

Willie Aames

Florence Henderson

Robert Pine

Ted Lange

Bob Barker

Art Linkletter

Ruta Lee

Alan Copeland

Peter Falk

Ron Masak

Norman Lloyd

Shirley Jean Measures

WALTER WINCHELL

Billy Barty is a honey.
He's a picture celebrity IN PERSON who has plenty to offer.
As a TRAP DRUMMER, he's a whiz.
As a COMEDIAN, he's a riot.
As a SINGER, he's captivating!
As an ACROBAT, he's a crackerjack.

PETER MARSHALL

The part I loved about Billy was how sometimes he seemed to forget that he wasn't five or six feet tall. For instance, while playing golf with him one day, he teed off and almost hit the ball the same distance I had (which was a very decent shot, I might add), and Billy truly could not understand why it didn't go over two hundred yards. He truthfully was baffled. Just like when he would step up to a podium that completely covered him up, and instead of asking to be raised to its level, he would just begin to talk behind the podium as if it were the correct size. Although that was in fun, I think he often had to remind himself that his size was different because his mind was just so tall. I loved him very much and think of him often, which always brings a smile to my face.

*Peter and Laurie Marshall, Buddy Ebsen, Jan and
Mickey Rooney, and Billy Barty.
Photo courtesy of Peter Marshall.*

PAT BOONE

I had a long, happy friendship with Billy, competing and partnering with him in many athletic events, always amazed at the physical abilities of this little giant.

The fondest and most unique memory I have, though, is when he joined me on stage in Vienna! I was doing a concert there with a full orchestra and sold-out opera house, and had a high temperature. Billy came back stage to see me (he was there for some other reason), and I asked him if he would help me with the song, "Speedy Gonzalez." He immediately, of course, said he would. As I sang this worldwide rock hit, at two crucial places, Billy ran on stage with a sombrero that was almost covering him completely and a serape wrapped around his diminutive body. It generally brought the house down! It was all impromptu, as he had never seen me do it before, yet he blended perfectly into my rendition of the song and provided the entertainment highlight of the evening. And by the way, when the show was over, my fever was gone! It was so typical of Billy—anything to help out a friend.

Pat Boone.
Photo courtesy of Pat Boone

JACK NARZ
(Announcer, Game Show Host)

We did the Spike Jones show in the fall of 1957, I think. Billy was part of the troupe and performed and sang. One of his specialties was doing "head spins" in time with some of the music.

It was at this time that I took Billy out to the Lakeside Golf Club where we played. Then we met the rest of the guys in the bar to shoot the breeze. Johnny Weismueller (Tarzan) picked Billy up and put him on top of the bar, which was all it took to turn Billy on. He did an act for about fifteen minutes, much to the amazement of all the members present.

We both belonged to a group called the "Hollywood Hackers." They were known as Hollywood's golfing ambassadors of goodwill. We played in tournaments all over the country and then did shows after dinner.

The club had as members: producers, directors, writers, musicians, comedians, actors, announcers, emcees, singers, and the whole spectrum of show business. The shows we did were of professional quality.

One time Billy was on and running a little too long, and the producer told me (I was the emcee at this event) to go out and get Billy off stage so we could get the rest of the show on. As I went on the stage, Billy knew why I was coming, and he began to swing the microphone in a circle by its cord.

The audience thought it was part of the act and started laughing at Billy holding me off with the swinging microphone. It ended up catching me along the side of the head and I went down like a felled tree.

Closest to the Green
Billy was unable to drive golf carts like the rest of the fellows sitting down, and so he stood up to drive them. The Hackers gave him two awards: the "Golf Cart Driver of the Year" award, and a trophy for being "Closest to the Green" at all times.

Jack Narz.
Photos courtesy of David Narz

DAVID NARZ

I'll always remember Billy, but two times in life especially.

A long time ago, back when everybody knew everybody, my father was the announcer on *The Bob Crosby Show.*

There was another gentleman with a little singing group named Alan Copeland who was also featured on this show.

Well, as our families grew close, we realized that Alan Copeland was married to Billy Barty's sister (Dede). We'd get together on holidays at the Copeland house out in the "Valley," and Billy would be there with his wife and kids. They would set up a ping-pong table on the back patio, and we would all try to beat Billy.

He would jump up on a chair so he could get a full swing in with the paddle and not hit his arm. Billy was the champ, although I suspect that on occasion he would let one of the kids win so he could get a drink or a bite to eat.

Billy Barty's Big Top

I remember also the *Billy Barty Big Top* show hosted by our surrogate father Billy, dressed like the ringleader at the circus. He'd run up and down the isles, introducing cartoons and entertaining the group in the big top.

Because I was raised around television personalities (my father is Jack Narz, his brother Jim Narz a.k.a. Tom Kennedy, and my other uncle is Bill Cullen), I met many other business relationships while visiting Dad as he would tape shows. But I think about those days in the back yard with Billy with much fondness, and being a kid during the years of Billy Barty, I wouldn't trade for all the reruns on Cartoon Network and Nickelodeon combined.

I only wish my kids had someone on TV who could look them in the eyes and say what he meant and live what he said.

David Narz family.
Debbie, David, Dustin, Dylan, and Derek Narz.
Photo courtesy of David Narz

MICKEY ROONEY

I worked as a child with Billy Barty, and found him to be a great friend and teacher. Even as a kid, he knew how to play a scene. He was very clever, and developed into a fine actor. He was my friend, and I will always miss him. Anybody who knew Billy knows he was a big man with a big heart. We remained friends even until the day he passed away.

Interview with Buck Wolf

In an interview with Buck Wolf of ABC Entertainment, Mickey states that "Billy was one of the funniest guys I ever worked with. I can't imagine what my life would have been like without Billy. He was one of a kind, and was very charitable." (Mickey had been home from the hospital only two days after undergoing multiple bypass heart surgery when he paid his last respects to Billy.) He commented, "I just had to be there."

JAN ROONEY

Courage, strength, love, warmth, and strong character are what Billy Barty was all about. Little did I know as a young girl watching *Billy Barty's Big Show* with Billy as the host that I would meet the man who gave so much to so many.

My husband Mickey Rooney introduced me to Billy, a man that I respect greatly.

Mickey took our son Mark to the "Little People's" golf tournament, and what a grand day they both had.

Years later, Billy would play a character in Mickey's western movie, *The Legend of O.B. Taggart.* I recall hours of fun and laughter on the phone talking to Billy about the many times he and Mickey shared growing up.

Billy was a hero to us all.

Mickey and Jan Rooney.
Photo courtesy of Jan and Mickey Rooney

Collage of Dick Clark, Tom Bosley, Pat Morita, Don Knotts.

DICK CLARK
(Dick Clark Productions)

Words cannot describe my total admiration for Billy Barty. Our paths crossed many times over the years, both personally and professionally, and he always left me inspired.

One second thought: his talent, determination, and spirit must have inspired all of us who were fortunate enough to have him as part of our lives.

TOM BOSLEY
(Happy Days, Father Dowling Mysteries)

In my eyes, Billy Barty was small only in stature. He was a giant filled with talent and had a purpose to his life that could teach many of us a lesson. He was extremely talented in his profession and generous in his demeanor.

I worked with him a couple of times, and always found the aura around him filled with laughter. He will be missed by all who knew him, and was a little guy that many looked up to.

PAT MORITA
(Arnold in *Happy Days, Karate Kid*)

Billy Barty may have been one of the world's "Little People," but he was, oh, so much more than that.

A Giant Life Force
Whenever I was around him, be it in front of or off the camera, he was a giant life force whose absence amongst us now leaves a giant void.

He was, in addition to being many things to many people, a talented, humorous, brainy, upstanding human being I was proud to know and call a warm, personal friend. Like the world, I miss you terribly, Billy.

DON KNOTTS
(The Andy Griffith Show)

One time, Billy and I were doing a television show and we had to go to the recording studio. I said "I don't have my car with me," and Billy said, "I'll drive you over!"

I said, "Waaaait a minute!"

But we got into his car with all those pedals elevated, and I rode with him in the front seat!

I remember Billy as being a really cheerful, upbeat guy to be around and very inspiring.

ED ASNER
(The Mary Tyler Moore Show)

Billy and I appeared one year on the Dodgers Celebrity baseball team. We were down in the locker room getting dressed. I had always thought of the "little people" as little people.

When I saw Billy undressed and saw how unbelievably equipped he was, I felt humbled and wanted to put on my street clothes and go home. I've always loved Billy Barty with his warmth and his giving.

Ed Asner
Photo courtesy of Ed Asner

BETTY WHITE
(The Mary Tyler Moore Show, Golden Girls)

Billy was a good friend for more years than I can count. No matter where we would see each other, he always left me smiling—or laughing.

He was a remarkable man and will long be remembered with great affection and respect.

Betty White.
Photo courtesy of Betty White

DICK VAN PATTEN
(Eight Is Enough)

I was such a fan of Billy's. He was one of the few kid actors who made the transition from child actor to adult, and he did it on pure talent.

I used to watch him on the Mickey McGuire series with Rooney. They were both such mature actors and could not say a line wrong.

I also remember how funny he was with Mary Tyler Moore on her show.

I miss him very much, and aside from his talent, he was also a very wonderful man.

Dick Van Patten.
Photo courtesy of Dick Van Patten

WILLIE AAMES

(Eight Is Enough, Charles in Charge, Bible Man)

I knew Billy from many guest appearances, golf tournaments, and parades.

Having grown up and spending thirty-three years in television, it is hard NOT to have been touched by Billy in some way.

Willie Aames.
Photos courtesy of Bibleman website

FLORENCE HENDERSON
(The Brady Bunch)

Billy Barty was a very unique human being. Born with challenges that would have stopped most people from pursuing any career, Billy chose one of the toughest careers—one in show business!

He just never let anything stop him.

I think everyone in our business knew and respected Billy. He was smart and he never complained. He loved his family and he was fearless.

Once we played together in a celebrity baseball game at Dodger Stadium. He was a "little person" only in stature. In every other way, he was a giant among men. It was a privilege to know him.

Florence Henderson.
Photo courtesy of Florence Henderson

ROBERT PINE
(CHiPs)

I remember once we were in Montgomery, Alabama, at the Governor's Mansion when George Wallace was governor.

George Lindsey (who played Goober in *The Andy Griffith Show*) had a celebrity golf tournament in which he raised funds for mentally retarded children for the George Lindsey Aquatic Center at the Alabama State Hospital.

Billy and I were both invited and attended the function. Even though we might not have agreed with Mr. Wallace politically, he was very nice to us.

We sat and shared a meal as well and joked with one another. I enjoyed his company very much. I looked forward to talking with Billy because I had never had an opportunity to earlier. Even though he played in an episode on *CHiPs,* I usually never had the same scenes as the guest stars.

I remember Billy mostly from a couple of golf tournaments that I was in, always being impressed with him and how he handled himself with his whole situation. He was a wonderful spokesman for little people, with a lot of dignity and class, and a nice sense of humor.

I have very warm remembrances of Billy with admiration, as everyone does.

Robert Pine.
Photo courtesy of Robert Pine

TED LANGE
(The Love Boat)

It was an honor for me to work with Billy during a *Love Boat* episode. He had long been a hero of mine. I will never forget when we had a scene together in the Pirates Cove Bar. We had some down time, and he and I got a chance to talk. We talked about the struggles we both shared in the business as minorities, and how determination plays a big factor in not giving up.

Billy and *The Wizard of Oz*

I asked if he had been in *The Wizard of Oz*. I assumed like most people that he must be in there somewhere, just as people assumed that I must have been in *Roots*. He told me he was not in the film, but that he knew a lot of people who had been in it, then he regaled me with stories that were passed on to him by some of his friends.

Grace and Dignity

What a great man to take the time to talk and share. We have had some other stars not quite so willing to share. It was refreshing to meet someone who treated everyone with grace and dignity. He will always be remembered by me as a true star.

Ted Lange.
Photo courtesy of Ted Lange

Bob Barker.

BOB BARKER
(The Price is Right, Truth or Consequences)

Billy Barty joined us on *Truth or Consequences* on several occasions, and without exception, he was a charming and hilarious guest.

He was surprisingly athletic, witty, and very quick with an ad-lib. The loss of this little man leaves a big void in our lives.

Art Linkletter, Ruta Lee, Shirley Jean Measures, Alan Copeland.

ART LINKLETTER

(Kids Say the Darndest Things)

I and all of us who knew Billy loved him very much indeed. He was a dear man and a gentle man.

RUTA LEE
(The Joey Bishop Show, Stage)

I was asked to do a classic stage show in the late sixties or early seventies for the San Bernadino Civic Light Opera. Having my name above the title meant that I had certain rights in casting. And the director with whom I had worked many, many times said, "I have an idea for the storyteller in this. I'd like you to think about using Billy Barty." I said, "Are you crazy? Billy Barty? I mean I adore Billy Barty, but this is going to become a cartoon! Yes, it's a comedy, but there are some serious poignant moments in it. How can you use Billy Barty? The broom that he has to use to sweep is three times as big as he is!"

The original role played on Broadway was done by Clyde Revell. He was a big, burly man as the storyteller, and here we are going to have a darling little person! It's going to be all wrong, all wrong! And I fought Jack tooth and nail. Then I finally gave in and said, "OK. I adore him—let's use Billy Barty." Jack ended up being right, God rest his soul. I cannot tell you how magnificent Billy was. He was the dearest, funniest, best character I have ever seen in my life. I enjoyed every single moment on and off stage with him. It just proves that you can have a wrong perception of something that is artistic. He was so marvelous, and the funniest picture of him in my mind is when he played the French Judge. Billy played about fifteen characters! So there he sits as the judge on the bench with those long wigged curls, and then lying on the bench with the curls hanging down on the ground in front of him and a gavel bigger than he was. It was the funniest scene I have ever seen! And he stole every minute from me and I could have hated him for it.

Billy also did several shows for me for the Thalians. When we honored Lucille Ball, he was one of our characters. I have a picture of Billy running across the stage chasing me with a lawnmower. He came to so many of our events.

The only thing that I've always regretted was that his tournament always fell at the time we were preparing for the Thalian Ball.

When I asked Ruta Lee when the first time she met Billy was, she said, "I think it was in the Garden of Eden. It has been so long. I've known him for so long it must have been when Adam and Eve were on the planet." I don't remember a time without Billy Barty!

Billy becomes your friend the minute you say "How do you do?" He worms his way into your heart, and I say he *does* because he still does. We are still seeing him on film on the large and small screens, and he is still getting into everybody's heart. I just loved Billy! Everybody did!

ALAN COPELAND

(Modernaires, Alan Copeland Singers, *Bing/Bob Crosby* and *Red Skelton Shows*)

Billy Barty was a multi-talented turned-on tempest in a teapot, bubbling over with heart, wit, and a Herculean determination to turn destiny's ill-dealt hand into a giant step for little people everywhere. As his sister Dede's husband for a pair of decades, I sat in on a chunk of this bantam heavyweight's life, always leaving his presence by the shot of his gentle ginseng.

A show-biz aspirant myself, I marveled at the humility of this luminous leprechaun, whose playful persona and awesome gymnastics helped make Busby Berkeley the wonder of Warner Brothers.

I know he is happy up there with Busby, scampering around through Dick Powell's legs, as the angels sing.

PETER FALK
(Columbo)

Whenever I ran into Billy, whether it was for five minutes or thirty, I always felt better when I left. There are some terrific people in the world, and Billy was one of them. But he was more than that—he was an inspiration.

Peter Falk.
Photo courtesy of Peter Falk

Ron Masak.
Photo courtesy of Ron Masak

RON MASAK
(Murder, She Wrote)

Short Jokes

As a friend of Billy's for over thirty years, he always asked me to play in and emcee his golf tournament. Of course we would set up all the "short" jokes.

"Billy, do short jokes bother you?"

Billy replied, "Not even a *LITTLE* bit."

Many years ago, when my twin boys were little tykes, Billy drove to my house. When he got out of that big car, my boys were amazed that a MAN who was the same size as they were was DRIVING a car.

One time Bill had called me to see if I would save him a drive to Dodger Stadium and deliver a letter that his ninety-year-old father had written to Tommy Lasorda to help stop a losing streak. Billy's dad Albert, a TALL man, had played baseball with Babe Ruth, so I happily delivered the letter.

Billy Barty was as large a talent as there was in show business, and his generous heart was even bigger.

Norman Lloyd.
Photo courtesy of Norman Lloyd.

Norman Lloyd

(Producer, Actor—Alfred Hitchcock brought him to Hollywood. He was the associate producer and later executive producer for *Alfred Hitchcock Presents*.)

Billy Barty once appeared for us on *The Alfred Hitchcock Hour*. It was a show called "The Jar." Pat Butram and Billy played in the opening scene in which the tone of the piece was established. I directed the show, and I'm here to tell you that to be the director of that scene was a piece of cake. There was no need for me to do anything but to sit back and enjoy. My point is that it is not often enough that we recognize actors like Billy. He is a performer of a special presence, and to honor him is to honor the talent, the skill, and the survivors of our profession.

A great American poet once wrote, "The purpose of any artist is to take life as he or she sees it and raise it to an elevated position where it has dignity." Billy has that quality of dignity, so that everything he does is an abiding interest. Many of us here have been in show business for a long time. One of the rewards is the pride we feel for fellow performers who have stayed the course. Billy Barty is such an actor. He belongs, and that is the most anyone can say of anyone in our profession.

SHIRLEY JEAN RICKERT MEASURES
(Little Rascals)

Billy and I grew up together and remained friends. My father drove my mother and me to an interview for the *Mickey McGuire Comedies* at Darmour Studios, and he waited in the car. Mom and I were in the studio for only a short time when Mom went rushing back to the car, dragging me behind her. Pop said, "Hon, what's the matter?" Mom said, "There is a baby in there that jumped out of a baby carriage and started doing cartwheels. *My* child can't do anything like that!" Pop talked her into going back in, and we found out later that it was Billy Barty! I was picked to play Tomboy Taylor in the series. He was the cutest little baby you've ever seen, but he was just a little older than I was at the time. I still can't do cartwheels!

Billy's entertainment collage.
Photos courtesy of Dede Barty Morse

Andy Williams.
Photo courtesy of Andy Williams

Orpheum.
Photo courtesy of Dede Barty Morse

Marquis.
Photo courtesy of Dede Barty Morse

Chapter Eight

COMEDIANS/IMPRESSIONISTS

John Byner
Bob Einstein
Fred Travalena
Marty Ingels/Shirley Jones
Ruth Buzzi
Red Buttons (Billy's Memorial)
Norm Crosby

John Byner, Bob Einstein, Fred Travalena, Marty Ingels, Shirley Jones

JOHN BYNER

(Impressionist, comedian)

I first met Billy on a Bob Hope special, and it was right after they did the movie *Jaws.* Since *Jaws* was a big hit, some writers thought it would be a great idea to have a show about a bunch of comics that get killed by the pool during a party.

I was one of the comics standing around the pool table, and I had to pick up Billy and put him on the pool table five or six times. I realized he was very short but he was very heavy.

He did my show ***Bizarre,*** which aired in Toronto, Canada, and I was in many of his golf tournaments. One night I invited him up to my place for dinner as we were both staying at the same hotel. We ordered room service.

Billy just flipped up the cushion on the small chair and sat there with the cushion at his back, and he was able to touch the floor with his feet now that he had flipped the cushion up.

It was a natural thing for him, and we just sat down and ate at the coffee table and watched television and talked about the ***Bizarre*** show that he came up quite often to do.

I loved Billy, and went to his seventieth anniversary at Universal and had a good time there while I sat at Bob Hope's table.

You just can't help but say ***cute*** when you think about Billy and what he did and how he spent his life.

BOB EINSTEIN

(Super Dave Osborne)

Anecdotes with Billy

The first time I met Billy was on *The Smothers Brothers Show* in 1969. I worked with him over an eleven-year period. He worked with me on the show *Bizarre* and on *Super Dave,* and had unbelievable professionalism.

Billy was such a trooper. When we set up the special effect to rain in one of our skits, our prop person, by a horrible mistake, put it on hot water. So here was Billy standing there with steam coming off his head and he never said a word. He just went on with his sketch and did it!

Bathrooms in Public Places

I asked Billy to name a problem that most little people have because I wanted to use it in a sketch. He said "bathrooms in public places!" So we set up a bathroom as if it were in an airport. The sinks were high and the toilets were high and the dryer was high. Basically everything in there was out of reach, and Billy went through it by himself with not much of a script. He was hysterical!

How Do You Do?

There was a time we had another little guy on the show and he was a bellhop in the Royal York Hotel. He drank an awful lot and didn't remember too much.

One morning he walked by Billy and I introduced them saying, "John, this is Billy Barty."

And John said "How do you do?"

Billy replied, "How do you do? We just had breakfast yesterday!"

Billy Stuck on the Balcony

Billy was late for a rehearsal, and he was never late. We went to his hotel room and pounded on the door and couldn't find him. Finally we heard him! His problem was he couldn't open the door.

He was stuck on the balcony screaming because he was late; however, he was laughing.

He Never Complained

Everything was such an effort for Billy and he made nothing of it, especially in the later years after he had the accident and his leg was bowed. Things were hard, but he would never complain. I think Billy out lived his expectation by many years. He just loved working.

One thing you will find out about Billy is that he was not controversial. I don't know anyone who could say anything bad about him. He didn't do drugs or drink. He was a just a good person.

FRED TRAVALENA

BILLY BARTY? WHAT AN AMAZING PRESENCE AND HEART!

Billy asked me for several years to appear in his Palm Springs, California, event (to raise funds for his "Little People" organization). There were phone calls, letters, etc., but each year that the request came to my attention, it was after things had been booked. I always promised Billy that I would someday keep the commitment.

While my wife Lois and I were attending a concert for a charity starring Natalie Cole, we drove up to the exclusive mansion in Beverly Hills, along with many of Hollywood's top visibility stars.

There was a red carpet, and each person had his or her picture taken upon arrival at the massive front entrance and before going inside for dinner and the concert.

As I made my way up to the front of the line and was literally next in line with my wife, I heard a voice say, "Guess who? So Fred, are you gonna be there this year or not?"

It was beloved Billy sitting on a brick wall behind me, dangling his feet and smiling. We laughed our heads off.

I said, "Boy, when you want something, you go for it!" He said, "So, who else?"

Well, I said yes to Billy's event and attended and performed, for which Billy gave me a video of the performance later that year.

After I finished my set, Billy came on stage and grabbed my hand and pulled me back out to the spotlight. He said, "Fred, you can't leave until you do it" (that is an impression of Billy). I of course complied, and it brought the house down.

Billy was a gift to all who knew him.

MARTY INGELS AND SHIRLEY JONES

We've known Billy since he was a "little thing." (I just had to get that one out, but I promised myself, it'd be the last.) Like everyone else, we have known Billy for about two thousand years. It just seemed as if he was always there, like your old Uncle Rudy or those gray fleece-lined slippers in the closet. The one thing we never understood was that "Little People" designation, but for the compact package, there was never anything little about *William John Bertanzetti*. Not his boundless heart, nor his brain, nor his spirit, nor his boundless energy, and more boundless love, nor his unyielding dedication to addressing America's myopic perception of his disparate brothers and sisters who have for all too long been unnumbered and invisible. Wherever you are, Mr. B., take one of your cute little bows. You have done what so many of the big guys could not. You have changed the face of things forever.

Ruth Buzzi.
Photo courtesy of Ruth Buzzi

Ruth Buzzi
(Laugh-In, Sesame Street)

I met Billy years ago and worked with him in a couple of movies as well as guest starring on several TV shows together. I remember he had me as one of the celebrities to go to a horse race. I'll never forget that night because they asked us if we wanted to get in the car that goes right onto the track. The car approaches really close to where the gates are going to open and the horses come out. Then the car drives away from them, but the horses are coming with those big nostrils and their wide eyes, and they are wild. All of a sudden, the car pulls off the side of the track, and as they pass you, it looks like they are flying in the air. So every time I see a horse race now, I think of the time Billy and I went to that one race. It was so dynamic, and so incredible.

Meeting Billy's Family
Going to Billy's home was very special to me. Even though I didn't stay too long, I was able to meet his family.

You Always Felt Comfortable
I've worked with a lot of little people, and when you were around Billy, you always felt comfortable. He had a remarkable presence that was wonderful to be around and had a wonderful personality. We always had fun and great conversations. I really loved Billy.

RED BUTTONS
(Comedian)

Dede told us at Billy's funeral that she went over to Red Buttons and introduced herself to him. Mr. Buttons had mentioned to her that he wanted to say something to the audience on behalf of Billy. She responded, "That would be fine." When he got up to speak, this is what he said:

Red Buttons at Billy's Memorial (paraphrased)

"At one particular time in my life, I didn't know Billy, but I did know him through his work. We were talking about doing a pilot together for a TV show many years ago. When it was around lunchtime, we went to the commissary at the studio. As we were sitting around talking about show business and everything, Billy asked me if I have ever seen his impersonation of John the Baptist. I looked up at him and said, 'What? I know people do Jimmy Cagney, Jimmy Stewart, and Humphrey Bogart, but I have never seen anyone do John the Baptist.' Billy asked, 'Would you like to see it?' I said, yes! Because he was small, he used the white table cloth with an empty plate and put his head on the plate."

NORM CROSBY

It is a pleasure to remember Billy Barty, because any thought of Billy always brings a smile and a chuckle. He was a joy to know and be with. I enjoyed making him laugh, and he never failed to do the same thing to me. I played in Billy's golf tournament and he played in mine. One time he grabbed the microphone during the awards ceremony and claimed the prize for being closest to the ground, so we gave it to him. Billy was a wonderful actor and a great human being. If he was disturbed at all about his size, he never let it show in his career or his social life. He was fun to work with and he will be sorely missed.

Norm Crosby.
Photo courtesy of Norm Crosby

Chapter Nine

DODGERS/SPORTS

Tommy Lasorda
Gil and Dee Stratton
Michael Copeland
Gary Owens

Tommy Lasorda.

TOMMY LASORDA
(Los Angeles Dodgers)

Although Billy was small in stature, he was big in character. I remember presenting him a wristwatch for attending every Hollywood Stars game since its inception. He loved coming to Dodger Stadium and playing with the Dodger players. He did so much for others, specifically, raising money for those who were less fortunate than he. I have yet to find someone who didn't like Billy. He was a man of class. He may be gone, but never forgotten.

Gil and Dee Stratton.
Photo courtesy of Dee Stratton

GIL STRATTON

Billy was an excellent athlete, playing good golf, shooting baskets, or whatever he tackled. However, when he reported for football practice while attending L.A. City College, the coach figured an easy way to discourage the little man without hurting his feelings.

The coach told Billy that he had to have a uniform to work out and practice with the team. Undaunted, Billy had his mother make him a football uniform and he became a member of the team, even earning a letter.

When LACC came down near the goal line, Billy would join the huddle and take the snap from the center. He would dive between the big center's legs into the end zone for a touchdown!

Truly, Billy was one of the world's Biggest "Little Men!"

A sports memory from Gil Stratton, during his forty-year CBS Sports career and also known as Cookie in *Stalag 17*.

DEE STRATTON

The first time I saw Billy, he was walking across the campus at L.A. City College with my good friend Harold Uplinger. Harold, who was six feet three inches tall, later went on to play basketball at LIU and in the NBA. The two of them were in serious discussion as if on the same level, eye to eye. Beautiful!

Gil Stratton and Billy playing golf.
Photo courtesy of Dee Stratton

KAREEM AND BILLY
by Michael Copeland

The Hollywood Shorties

When I was about twelve years old, Uncle Billy arranged a special day for my younger brother Rick and me to meet "Little Oscar" and his Wienermobile in Los Angeles. I didn't know it at the time, but it was Jerry Maren who played Oscar Mayer's mascot and drove around the southern California area pitching their hot dogs and meat products. Billy and Jerry were good friends, and so we would see Jerry every so often when Billy was doing something special. One instance was the time not much later when he brought Jerry as a member of the "Hollywood Shorties" baseball team to our little league to play an "exhibition" game against our all-star team. They were hilarious and athletically competitive at the same time.

Imagine, if you can, a much smaller baseball version of the Harlem Globetrotters doing slapstick stunts, jokes, and gags. One stunt they choreographed was when they had the bases loaded. After the batter hit the ball, all of the "Shorties" ran to the opposite base across the diamond and ended up slamming into each other on the pitcher's mound! It took everybody by surprise!

Billy was always keeping my mom and his nephews in mind when something of significance was happening that he knew we would enjoy.

Dodger Stadium

I remember my mom telling my brother and me that Billy had invited us to watch him play baseball at Dodger Stadium. She said that there was going to be a game before the Dodgers played. The "Sportscasters" team was playing the "Hollywood Stars" team. So, for a couple of little league kids like my brother and me, this was exciting news.

I can remember when the announcer introduced Billy, who was coming in to pitch for the Hollywood Stars team. Kareem Abdul Jabbar was also on the team. So here's Uncle Billy letting go of his first pitch from the mound with a big wind-up.

The ball makes it across the plate okay, but the only problem was, it was on one bounce. The umpire calls it a ball. Then Billy goes into five hilarious minutes of arguing with the umpire.

Of course, to get the upper hand, Billy first called Kareem over to the mound. He got on Kareem's shoulders, and Kareem carried him over to argue that the pitch was a strike. He was quoted as telling the umpire that it didn't matter if it was on one bounce: the pitch still went **"right over the plate!"**

Gary Owens.
Photo courtesy of Gary Owens

GARY OWENS
(Laugh-In)

Billy Barty was a great pal of mine for many years. From 1968–1998, we always were a significant part of the Dodger Celebrity Baseball game at Dodger Stadium in Los Angeles.

He was always the consummate professional, always on time and a great crowd pleaser.

Usually he and Kareem Abdul Jabar would have a "let's pretend" fight at first base, with Billy kicking dirt on Kareem's shoes!

We did a lot of TV shows together, including *Games People Play* on TV, where Billy's basketball team played the coaches and beat them.

As Far as Entertainment?
We had a great time doing the movie *Diggin' up Business* together.

Joking with Billy
Billy was always inspirational and a great guy. Anytime he had a charity event, he would be my guest on my national radio show. One of my jokes that Billy loved was "Billy may be a little late today; he was injured while bungee jumping off the curb!" We did cartoon voices together and always spoke about his fun days with Spike Jones, where Billy did a killer impression of Liberace.

A Better Place
He was a man of tremendous talent and energy, and he made the world a better place.

Dodgers Celebrity photo
Ron Masak, John Ritter, Ed McMahon,
Gary Owens, Harvey Korman, and Billy Barty
Photo courtesy of Gary Owens

Hollywood Stars Night.
Photo courtesy of Gary Owens

Billy sports collage.

Chapter Ten

PACIFIC PIONEER BROADCASTERS
TRIBUTE TO BILLY BARTY
(Courtesy of Marty Halperin)

Patty Maloney
Jane Withers
Donald O'Connor
Tim Conway
Milton Berle
Steve Allen
Rodney Bardin
Fred Sutton
Marty Halperin
Marty Krofft
Ralph Edwards

PATTY MALONEY
(Actress, Billy's wife on *Little House on the Prairie*)

I met Billy when he was with Spike Jones. I came out to California when I was living in New York, and Billy was the first movie star that I ever dated. As I went back to New York, I said I would never, ever date another movie star! About twenty years ago, I wrote a letter to Billy and said I wanted to get back into show business. Within two weeks, I had a call from Sid and Marty Krofft that Billy had recommended me for a show. It was that incident that brought me back to California. I came out here with $500.00 in my pocket, and because of Billy Barty, I am still in California. Billy, you are an amazing human being. It takes a lot in this town to keep oneself in the business, and it takes an extremely huge human being to help someone else in her career. Billy Barty is that human being, and I'm the person that he helped.

JANE WITHERS
(Actress, Entertainer, Josephine the Plumber)

In 1933, there was a parade of all kinds of kids, and all of them wanted to be in the movies and were very talented.

Billy was the director of the Hollywood Baby Orchestra. It was so extraordinary to me to see this wonderful little person directing this enormous orchestra and doing it brilliantly! He didn't miss a note. That was my first introduction to Billy Barty. Many years passed, but I remember vividly the Mickey McGuire comedies because I did a radio show that was on every Saturday night and was paid $6.00 a performance. At the same time, I did a part as a black-faced angel for Warner Brothers, and I was swinging up on the wires and kept yelling to the assistant director, "Sir, what time is it? I've got to get to my radio show and it's live and I have to get out of here."

The reason I remember that so well is that night Billy Barty was one of the guests. I was so excited because I said, "That's the same person that directed this wonderful orchestra, and I had seen him in some of the Mickey McGuire pictures!" (Mickey Rooney was often on my radio program.)

Billy and I had many years of a very special friendship. He's a gentleman, the kindest, most gentle soul who has also been a wonderful father. I am so proud of what he's done for the little people. I love him very much. You know how they say that big things come in small packages? Well I have to say the greatest come in small packages in Billy Barty. I love you very much, and thank you for sixty-five years of friendship.

DONALD O'CONNOR
(Comedian, Singer, Dancer, Movies)

Boxing with Billy

Billy and I used to box together at the YMCA. The hardest I was ever hit was by this guy, because I had to get down on my knees, and the idea to not get hit in the ring is that you have to bounce around a lot. Because I was on my knees, I couldn't get away from him.

The Paladium in London

We had a lot of fun together, but the highlight of my career was when we worked together at the Paladium in London. It was a great experience. And as was said about being a consummate actor, Billy is about one of the ten greatest actors who ever lived. My favorite portrayal that Billy did was in *W.C. Fields and Me*. Billy has the greatest personality in the world. You know, the most difficult thing about a person who is known for personality, for an actor, is he must lose that and have to become the character himself. Billy submerges his own personality and has never done a lousy performance in his life. He doesn't know how.

Honesty

We have been pals for over sixty years. I tell you one of the greatest qualities about Billy that I can think of is the fact that he is so very, very honest.

I love Billy, and I always have!

TIM CONWAY

You asked me to send a note, and this is a note. If you asked me to send him a car, I would have sent him a car.

Billy and I did a series together called *Ace Crawford, Private Eye,* and it only lasted five weeks. I still believe deep in my heart that it was his fault we went off the air!

Billy, you've always been a favorite of mine.

MILTON BERLE

Billy Barty is the sweetest, gentlest man I ever knew.

STEVE ALLEN

Billy Barty is a man I have always **looked up** to (which isn't easy).

RODNEY BARDIN
(Radio Host)

One day in the nineties, I saw a new show called *Short Ribbs* starring Billy Barty. It was a show with little people as the actors doing skits and stunts, and had the look of an early *Saturday Night Live.* At the same time, I had just started a radio talk show in Los Angeles called **"At a Glance"** with Rodney Bardin. I was the host, producer, and director. After seeing *Short Ribbs* again, I thought it would be fun to have Billy on my show. So I called KDOC TV 56 and asked for Billy. To my surprise, they put me through. He answered the phone with a gruff voice and listened to what I had to say. I could hear in the background the director calling him. Billy said, "Call me at my home office tonight." That night I did just that. Billy answered the phone, and we began a dialog about my show. I explained to him that he would be the **first celebrity** I would interview. "I would love to do the show," he said. We set up a date. The show would be recorded in Hollywood at the American Radio Network. It was pouring rain, with flooded streets, and it was cold. Time came to do the show, and no Billy. Now I was getting a bit worried. At 10:15 a.m., I called him at home. He answered the phone half-asleep. I said, "Billy, it's Rodney at the radio station. Are you able to come?" He said, "I am so sorry; I forgot. I will leave right now." He showed up fifteen minutes later, and we began the program. Everyone at the station was in awe that I was able to get such a big star on my little and yet new show. He told me a few stories about the time he traveled with Spike Jones. He said, "We did not have much money in those days, and Spike would take me to the movies and say, 'one adult and one child,' and so we went in. And to save money on a train, Spike would put me in a suitcase and take me on for free." During a commercial break I told the audience, "We will be right back with actor **Billy Bardin**."

Just then the crew started to bust up, and Billy almost fell out of his chair. Like a true professional, we came back and Billy said, "Billy here—I straightened Rodney out on his name."

I received more mail about that show than any other, and ten years later, it is still my best. After the show, we took pictures in the studio. The studios are small and I had to hunch down. I am six feet four inches tall, so the picture is mostly of me contorted. I walked him out to his car and it was still pouring rain. The curb became a river. He looked up at me and said, "Could you carry me across? I might drown!" So I did, and he was heavier than he looked. We were very well acquainted, and I visited him at his home and office many times.

In 2000, the founder of the Long Beach International Film festival told me about an award they wanted to give out. I recommended that it should go to Billy Barty. They checked on him and found out about the wonderful things that he did. The award is called *"The Billy Barty Humanitarian Award."* Billy was the *first* to get it. Many of his friends came to the show along with his wife Shirley, Supervisor Mike Antonovich, and Super Dave Osborne. It was not long after that he went into the hospital. I spoke to him while he was in there and he was in good spirits. Just before Christmas I received the dreaded call that he had passed. I had many tears in my eyes as I started to reflect on the past and the many things that he had done. He brought joy to millions of people. At least a thousand people went to his funeral, friends and fans alike. Long-time friends such as Mickey Rooney, Donald O'Connor, Mike Antonovich, and so many more were there. These were sad times, but his antics will live forever.

FRED SUTTON
(Old friend and scholarship chairman of the Billy Barty Foundation)

In 1946, I just got out of the Marine Corps and I was at my first day on campus at Los Angeles City College. All of a sudden, a little person rides by on a bicycle with a letterman's sweater on from a football team at LA City College. Billy and I were both journalism majors so we became very good friends. We had played on the first basketball team, and he was one of the best golf putters that I have ever seen.

MARTY HALPERIN

I always wanted to have something to do with radio, so I ended up taking a class at L.A. City College in 1945. At the start of the class, we had to get up in front of a microphone. I was supposed to read a little drama, but I didn't pay too much attention to it. While I was speaking at the mike, out of the corner of my eye I saw a chair moving. I thought to myself, "What the heck is that?" It then moved around to the other side of the microphone, and suddenly Billy hopped up on the chair and started facing me. He began reading his part, and I read mine. That is how we first met. I was drafted after that semester, and went in the armed forces radio services and spent time there as a recording engineer. After I left the service, I went back to City College and radio, and of course I saw Billy there. When I graduated from City College, I went on to LA State. The schools were on the same campus. Billy and I were both actively involved in student government, so our paths crossed all the time. He played football and basketball, and from what I understand, they had five plays all designed around him. The first time the other team saw him they thought it was a joke, until they saw him in uniform having the ball and running towards the goal line.

MARTY KROFFT

(Creator of fourteen children's shows such as *H.R. Pufnstuff,* *Sigmund and the Sea Monsters,* and *The Bugaloos*)

I met Billy in the late sixties, and we go back a long way. When I think of all the joys and all of the heartaches I've had in this business, as I think of Billy, I think of the *joys*. He is the ultimate professional and ultimate talent. Everybody wants to be in show business, but nobody wants to feel the pain. Whenever Billy showed up, there wouldn't be any trouble. He kept it all together and really helped us a lot. I'll never forget him for it.

RALPH EDWARDS
(*This is Your Life* TV series)

Billy Barty is a long-time friend of everyone, a super athlete and a God-given performer, exuding fellowship wherever he goes. Thirty-three years ago on March 30, 1960, I had the honor of presenting Billy Barty with his *This is Your Life* to America. We repeated it six months later because it was so darn good. It is one of the greatest *This is Your Life* shows that we have done. It hasn't lost its spirit, nor has Billy. All the members of the Pacific Pioneer Broadcasters revere you and are proud to present to you their outstanding achievement award. This silver plate is in honor of your remarkable contribution to us and the world.

Chapter Eleven

FAMILY MOMENTS

Christine Piper (Billy's niece)
Rick Copeland (Billy's nephew)
Michael Copeland (Billy's nephew)
Lori Neilson (Billy's daughter)
David Neilson (Billy's son-in-law)

Rick, Michael, and Christine Copeland
(Billy's nephews and niece)

Piper family.

CHRISTINE PIPER

Thinking of my Uncle Billy brings a colorful wave of experiences, memories, family, and professional encounters to mind.

His arms held me when I was a baby, and his words guided me as I grew from a child to a woman. Because of his belief in me, I've been part of an expansive library of projects on behalf of individuals with disabilities.

There he was speaking at a Rotary meeting, sitting at a table with a diverse group sharing a common goal, producing a video capturing the signing of the Americans with Disabilities Act, and sending a video crew to Washington, D.C., on the first Barrier Awareness Day.

They visited the Vice President (Dan Quayle) and legislators at the Capitol on behalf of people with disabilities.

Needing a video producer fast, within a day or two, Uncle Billy had introduced them to me and to my work, and had me on the phone to the camera crew.

At this moment I am still working for the same California State Department that provided the production work for that video, the California Department of Developmental Services.

Thanks to Billy, my mind and heart have been opened to see the abilities and the heroism of the people that I have had the pleasure to meet in my work.

As for Uncle Billy, I never thought of him having a disability, he was just—well, my Uncle Billy.

Rick, Linda, Rachel, and Sam Copeland.

"WHEN UNCLE BILLY BAILED ME OUT OF CUSTOMS."
by Rick Copeland

Heathrow Airport

I am Billy Barty's nephew Rick. One time I went to England, and upon arriving at Heathrow Airport, I was sporting shoulder-length hair with a guitar in tow. No sooner did we touch ground when the Heathrow police were asking me questions such as, "What do you plan on doing during your stay in England?" And, "You're not going to play for money in London, are you?" I must have said the wrong thing or something because they thought I looked pretty suspicious. It seemed to me that they had every intention of deporting me. Minutes turned into hours. Thirteen hours passed before they bused me along with a bunch of deportees from the Middle East for a bite to eat. It consisted of two pieces of white bread, margarine, an apple, and a cup of tea.

Help! Uncle Billy?

By this time I was freaking out! I kept telling them to call my Uncle Billy because he was starring in a film with Tom Cruise called *Legend.* He would explain that I was there only on holiday! After the meal was over (which I did not eat), we returned to the airport only to find my Uncle Billy waiting for me, not too happy I might add, but forgiving. Vouching for me and promising the authorities I wouldn't seek work in the United Kingdom, they let me go in his custody. Yea! We dined in the most incredible restaurants and took in the openings of the musicals *Cats, Little Shop of Horrors,* and *Starlight Express.*

This will always be the story I will tell my children when they ask me about my Uncle Billy.

the Road Scholars

Michael and Debra Copeland and granddaughter Tiffany Rep

"MY UNCLE BILLY"
Michael Copeland

When I was about eight years old, I can remember my mother bringing my brother Ricky and me over to the Barty house at 946 Normandie Street in Los Angeles. They had a three-bedroom white house where she grew up and her parents still lived. That is where I met "Billy Barty," whom my mother introduced as "Uncle Billy." Although I noticed that he was small, my grandfather, my grandmother, Aunt Evy, and Mother never treated "Uncle Billy" any different than any other "normal person." So I didn't treat him any different either. It would become very obvious once my grandfather asked him to spin on his head that he was not a "normal person," but a very special and talented person in a small body. Uncle Billy showed my younger brother Ricky and me how to shoot a basketball, as well as throw, hit, and catch a baseball along with playing football. He also taught me how to hold drum sticks, which later was very prophetic as I went on to be a professional drummer, touring the United States.

Neilson family.
Albert, Ellen, Billy, Shirley, Lori, and Braden Barty
Photo courtesy of Dede Barty Morse

LORI BARTY NEILSON

I remember my dad taking me to school on the first day of kindergarten. He was told that I belonged in a school for the handicapped because I was a dwarf.

My father said, "No way." He fought and got me in that school. He never let me do anything less than anyone could do, whether they were four feet, six feet, or ten feet tall.

DAVID NEILSON
(Billy's son-in-law)

I was born to average-sized parents back when no one knew much about dwarfism. The doctor told my mother that I wouldn't live past three, and that I wouldn't walk or talk.

One day she took us to see Billy's TV show, and he saw me in the audience and came over to talk to us. When my mother told him what the doctor said, Billy said the doctor was stupid. He gave my mom his telephone number and told her if she ever needed help or just needed to talk to him, to call.

That was the kind of man he was. My mom was shocked, but I think she was even more shocked years later when I wound up marrying his daughter Lori.

Billy, Albert, Ellen, Shirley, Braden, and Lori Barty

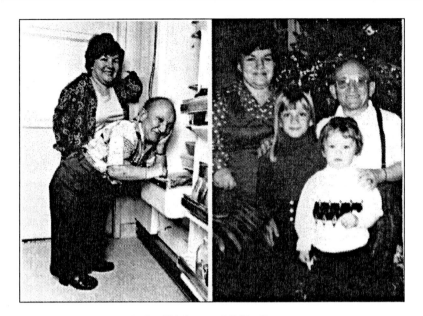

Left: Shirley and Billy Barty.
Right: Shirley, Lori, Billy, and Braden Barty.
Photo courtesy of Dede Barty Morse

Chapter Twelve

BILLY BARTY'S MAGIC VOICE

Catherine Parkins
T.J. Figment

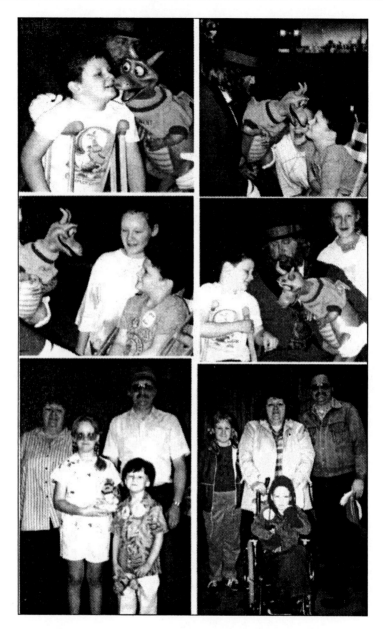

Catherine, Nancy, Craig, and Erik Parkins.
Photo courtesy of Catherine and Nancy Parkins

CATHERINE PARKINS

In 1986, there was a five-year-old boy in Michigan whose life was drastically changing. This pre-schooler was learning first-hand what cancer meant. He was discovering that his innocent world was about to be turned upside down. This little boy, Erik Parkins, who loved racing his toy cars and playing hide and seek, and who was content digging in a dirt patch in his front yard for hours, had to have his left leg amputated below the knee because he had a mysterious disease called muscle cancer (rhabdomyosarcoma). He lost all of his dark brown hair to chemotherapy treatments. In 1986 Erik was in the hospital, and all of five years old wondering why he had to have cancer and wondering if he would live or die. He had stopped eating, stopped smiling, stopped laughing, and stopped reacting to the world around him. Depressed, he had stopped living. The world he had known was gone. What do children wish they could do when they know they are faced with death? What can possibly make them smile again? Erik's mother, Nancy, phoned the Make-A-Wish Foundation of Michigan to find out if he qualified for a wish from the organization. One of Erik's dreams was to meet Mickey Mouse. The Disney characters, of course, are the opposite of disease, of a hospital, and of reality. His wish was granted in January 1987, and the entire family was sent to Walt Disney World for a one-week vacation. Erik's condition was so poor at this point that he should have been taken to a hospital rather than to Florida. Not knowing the wish could be rescheduled, Erik and his family flew to Walt Disney World. The itinerary sent the family to EPCOT Center upon their arrival on Tuesday even though Erik's wish was to meet Mickey Mouse.

They'd been to only an attraction or two before Erik needed to go to First Aid, as he didn't feel well. Even the Disney magic, it seemed, was not enough to brighten Erik's spirit. Then, the family went to the *Journey into Imagination* pavilion, sponsored by Kodak. What transpired was nothing short of magical. In the original *Journey into Imagination* ride, visitors met Dreamfinder, who piloted his "Dream Machine" through the sky, searching for sources of imagination. Along the ride, he introduced his friend, Figment.

Figment, a purple dragon, with a scratchy voice and child-like inno-
cence, popped out of the "Dream Machine," and Erik laughed for
the first time in months. Two days later, Erik asked for scrambled
eggs at the hotel restaurant, after not having eaten solid food for two
months. On the Sunday following the Make-A-Wish trip to Florida,
Erik ate six dinner-sized plates of scrambled eggs. From seeing
Figment at EPCOT Center, Erik had re-discovered his will to live.
His oncology doctor could not believe the change in Erik's health
and attitude. In May 1987, the family returned to Walt Disney
World for a vacation that Erik could enjoy as a five-year-old who
could walk and run with a prosthetic leg, and who was becoming a
typical little boy again. Of course, Erik wanted to first visit *Journey
into Imagination* so he could see Figment. After one year of
chemotherapy, Erik was declared 99.9 percent cured by his doctor.
He remained cancer-free for two years, before it came back with a
vengeance. The cancer had relapsed in his leg, groin, and lungs after
a misdiagnosis. As Erik continued to battle cancer over a six-year
period, he visited Figment a total of twelve times. With each visit,
Erik would find strength and courage to fight the cancer and live.
Figment served as a symbol for Erik. Figment plush would go into
surgery and chemotherapy treatments with him.

At one point, seventy-six Figment toys, plush, and figurines were
on display in the house. Erik loved Billy Barty, not realizing that it
was he who gave Figment life through his voice. For Erik, Figment
was real. Still, without knowing why he liked it, Erik would watch
UHF over and over because he loved Billy Barty's character and his
antics in the movie. Erik would also watch the episodes of *Little
House on the Prairie* where Billy Barty was the guest star. In both
cases, Erik didn't realize why he was attracted to those shows. He
didn't realize he was hearing Figment's voice. We are so grateful
that Billy Barty performed as Figment's voice, because it was
through his words as he popped out of the "Dream Machine" that
inspired Erik and helped him to live again. Given the sort of cancer
Erik had, his doctors had said he should not have lived the six extra
years he did. They attributed Figment's magic to Erik's continued
longevity. I always loved Billy Barty. When I found out he was the
person who gave life to Figment, it made me even happier. That day

in *Journey into the Imagination* when Erik laughed, I began to cry. You see, Santa Claus had literally dropped his sleigh in our living room that Christmas and that didn't even faze Erik. But when Figment popped out of the Dream Machine and spoke, it sparked him. I had written Billy a thank you letter. He called me, but I was at work at the Disney store and missed the call. Although we never were able to make the connection, just knowing he phoned was more than enough.

T.J. FIGMENT
("Figment" webmaster)

I still remember someone e-mailing me the news about Billy's death shortly after December 24, 2000. Upon hearing that, it felt as if "Figment" was now completely gone. I posted a page with Billy's photos and biography two months after his death. Many people were enchanted to find out that the voice behind "Figgie" was actually Billy Barty. Sadly, many people said it was depressing to hear about his death, and my page took the light-hearted, jolly feel away from the rest of the website. Shortly thereafter, I removed the page. Now I would like to stick a page back up there called "The Voice Behind "Figment," which would more or less celebrate his accomplishments. Even though Disney now has brought the little dragon back to the spotlight in the *Journey into Imagination* ride at EPCOT, I know it won't quite sound like the "Figment" we all know and love. Billy was indeed a man of many talents, and I am convinced that "Figment" wouldn't have been 'Figment" without him. www.figmentsimagination.com.

Chapter Thirteen

FANS

Cindy
Knit-O-Matic
Laura Corsini
Debbie Chaffee

WITH ETERNAL ADMIRATION, CINDY

Dear Mr. Barty:

I was born in a small town near Birmingham, Alabama. When I was four years old, my parents started drinking. My parents had always been strict, but things started getting really tough. It went from spankings to beatings, first with belts, then electric cords and other various objects, and finally with the fist. It always caused me a lot of problems because I was a good little girl. I got straight A's in school and was respectful and kind to others. It was always embarrassing to go to school with black eyes and a broken nose, saying I'd fallen down or walked into a wall. When I was ten, the sexual abuse started and continued until I left when I was fifteen. I spent a long time wondering why. I blamed myself, so needless to say I thought I was a really bad person. That's all changed now. I've been in therapy for about a year. I have what they call Post Traumatic Stress Syndrome. I thought it was a disease only Vietnam Vets got. It really surprised me that I was reacting normally to my extreme situation. The most rewarding part of my therapy has been my group sessions, with people that have similar problems. Not all of them are doing as well as I, but we all try to help each other. There are three guys from the war who are really having problems. I know it would help them tremendously if you would sign a photo for them. It would show them somebody of great importance cares for them. I know how rare it is for God to make a beautiful person like you and I am personally grateful for His wisdom. A thousand years from now, people will know your name. That must be a really good feeling.

With eternal admiration,
Cindy.

"Knit-O-Matic"

Billy influenced so many children in his lifetime that many of them in their forties and fifties still remember the impact he had on them. You will see in the following story that a simple Knit-O-Matic and the kindness Billy had shown a little girl meant so much to her that at the time of Billy's passing, she was prompted to send us her memory of him.

I have always been such a huge fan of Billy Barty. I watched his kiddy show in the sixties religiously, and remember when he brought his wife and daughter on the program. He was ahead of his time in enlightening kids about people who were different. I was fascinated by his size as a child, and I appreciate now (as an adult) being able to see someone who was physically different than I was. He never seemed odd to me, but how great it was to have an adult who was my size (actually smaller). I went to the program with my Brownie troop in 1967 when I was eight years old and ended up being a contestant. My name was drawn to play the surprise prize at the end of the show. I used to watch the program every day with my brother, and we were fascinated with the array of prizes that could be won. We always made fun of the kids who wanted to win the bike as greedy, and thought that the big loser prize was the Scrabble game (too intellectual). Mr. Barty would turn a card with the name of a toy on it until you said "Stop," then you win the next prize in the stack of cards. I had my heart set on the Knit-O-Matic (sort of an automatic knitting machine). The way the game was structured, you couldn't win the first prize in the stack. Wouldn't you know, the first card had the Knit-O-Matic! I was really nervous, and I was sure that I was letting too many cards get turned over, so I finally yelled **"Stop,"** and guess what I won? The Scrabble game! Oh well.

When the show was over, Mr. Barty lovingly took me by the hand over to the table with the prizes. He handed me the Scrabble game and the Knit-O-Matic! I never forgot that. It made such a huge impression on me. I must add, however, the Knit-O-Matic never worked, and I think we still have that Scrabble game around some-where. Billy Barty will always be in my heart for making my fifteen minutes of fame so sweet.

Laura Corsini.

LAURA CORSINI
My special day!

It was my birthday (I think it was my eighth) and I was with my older sister. My dad knew Billy Barty and his friend Jerry Maren, the one who played Oscar Mayer. That is how I was able to get on the Billy Barty Big Show. I was so excited about going on the show on *my birthday*! I didn't know about it until that very day, but I knew you got a lot of cool stuff when it was your birthday! I absolutely loved Billy Barty, and I never missed that show! When we got to the studio, and they seated us and prepared us to go live, my dad came up to tell us that Billy Barty wouldn't be there that day because he was across the street filming a movie with Elvis Presley. Oh my gosh! You can imagine the disappointment of a small child who was so looking forward to meeting Billy Barty on her birthday. There was only one other person that I would have been as happy to meet other than Billy Barty, and that was Elvis Presley! Yes, even at that age I was also a big Elvis fan. After that they had a hard time keeping me on the seat. I wanted to run as fast as I could, and I remember crying while wondering why we just couldn't go over there. That is all I wanted to do. Hobo Kelly was there that day as the substitute host and she interviewed me on television and gave me all kinds of great things, but I kept trying to say I wanted to go across the street! Needless to say, they didn't let me talk much, but they kept giving me a lot of stuff. Here it is today, thirty-five years later, and I still love Elvis Presley and Billy Barty. I can't ever eat a Rold Gold pretzel without thinking about that special day where I missed meeting my two special heroes. Many kids at my school saw the show and I was quite the celebrity when I returned the next day! Kids thought I was cool, but nobody seemed to understand my disappointment. My dad took me many times after that to meet Oscar Mayer, but it wasn't quite the same as meeting Billy Barty or Elvis Presley!

I was able to ride in the Wienermobile and I have a drawer full of the original Oscar Mayer Weenie Whistles and Wienermobile trucks, but I'm sorry to say I was never able to meet Billy Barty! I've spoken to many of my old friends from back then, and asked them if they remembered the show. Considering their ages, people in their mid-forties, they get a look of wondrous childlike twinkles in their eyes, and their voices have a childlike ring to them when they say, "Yeah! Billy Barty? I remember him!" My son, who is now twenty-one and in the USMC, refers to Billy Barty as his grandpa's friend.

MY EXPERIENCE WITH BILLY BARTY
By Debbie Chaffee

I first saw Billy Barty when I was five years old. At that time we lived across the street from Buena Park High School in California. I remember one day my brothers dragging me across the busy street to the school and sitting in this enormous auditorium.

Then, the lights went low and I saw a person who looked about my height but was an adult! Wonder of wonders to my five-year-old mind! I had never seen a short-statured person before.

When Mr. Barty approached the podium, everyone was clapping and laughing as he looked around him. He glanced up at the impossibly high podium, grabbed a chair, and then clambered on top.

When I was fifteen, I had the honor of meeting him in person. He shook my hand, but unfortunately I was in costume this time as Chuck E Cheese. It was the opening of Billy Barty's Roller Fantasy in downtown Fullerton. I went to the rollertorium every weekend that summer, not just because I loved skating, but hopefully to meet Mr. Barty again. I wanted to shake his hand with my un-costumed one and tell him how he opened my eyes to small people. You see, even though I am of normal stature, I was always shorter than most kids my age, which made me rather insecure and shy for most of my childhood and teenage years. The last time I saw him before his death was in the Strawberry Festival Parade, when he was the Grand Marshall. He certainly was grand and I explained to my then eight-year-old son what a great man he was, in that small now frail form.

I admired him for his determination and great work by making other small people a part of the human race and of course for his open, warm smile that never seemed to fade as the years went on.

I wept when I heard he died, as it seemed to me that people like him were somehow magical and should live forever.

QUOTES FROM BILLY BARTY

What do you think the two most important, influential, and appreciated words in our daily vocabulary are?

Thank you!

I have a feeling that we have been placed on this earth for a special reason, and although I have not fulfilled all my missions, I am trying.

I have been truly blessed from the man upstairs.

I think we should bring back the three R's to our country. That's RESPECT, RESPONSIBILITY, and RELIGION.

1924–2000